NAVIC

CLICKETY-CLACK

NAVIGATING THE CLICKETY-CLACK

How to Live a Peace-Filled Life in a Seemingly Toxic World
Volume 3

Featuring:
International Bestselling Authors
Michael Beckwith, Dr. John Demartini, and Keith Leon S.

Also Featuring:
Contributing Authors—Christina Frazier, Lianne Hofer, Inge Jechart,
Erin Kinney, Julianna Jaffe Leven, Mike Mantic, Annabelle Merriman,
Randall Monk, Jason Michael Powers, Heather Grace Powers, Lori Shen,
Genevieve Siegel, Sarah Spann, Steph St. Amand, Laurie St Clare,
Trey Stinnett, Nicole Thibodeau, Marie-Laure Will, and Gretchen Wilson

BEYOND
BELIEF
—PUBLISHING—
YOU HOLD THE FUTURE IN YOUR HANDS

ISBN: 978-1-945446-15-3

Rev. Michael Beckwith / Fletch Rainey

*This book is dedicated to our dear friend and spiritual mentor,
Fletch Rainey. RIP, dear Fletch. May your teachings about
the Clickety-Clack live on and serve humanity
for many years to come.*

Praise for
Navigating the Clickety-Clack
Volume 3

"Living a more peaceful life is easy when you take the advice of these bestselling and featured authors. In this book, you'll learn different ways these authors view and deal with their respective challenges. You will feel uplifted and supported by reading it."

~ Bob Proctor, Bestselling Author and Speaker
Featured Teacher from the hit movie, *The Secret*

"After twenty-eight years of being in the field of medicine, I have concluded that the happiest, healthiest, and most prosperous people are those who know and practice the skill of returning to calm and centeredness, no matter what's going on in their lives. *Navigating the Clickety-Clack, Volume 3* shares a generous smorgasbord of simple yet effective tools and strategies to do just that. I highly recommend you add this precious book to your healing toolbox!"

~ Karen Kan, MD, Doctor of Light Medicine
Founder of the Academy of Light Medicine

"Each page of this book carries with it ageless wisdom, truth, and the encouragement needed to navigate through even the most seemingly toxic situations."

~ Gwen Lepard, Speaker and International Bestselling Author

"Each of us is a Masterpiece. *Navigating the Clickety-Clack* helps us realize this truth and guides us in living from our sacredness.

Joy, grace, and peace then permeate our lives and fuel love beyond words. Give yourself and those you love the gift of this book!"
~ Dr. Kymn Harvin, Author of *The Soul of America Speaks: Wisdom for Healing and Moving Forward*

"So many pearls of wisdom in this book! *Navigating the Clickety-Clack* is a must-read for anyone seeking to create a happier, healthier, more peaceful life."
~ Cristina Smith, Award Winning, Bestselling Author of the *Yoga for the Brain* series

"This book is filled with wisdom, guidance, inspiration, and insights that are guaranteed to help anyone who is trying to *Navigate the Clickety-Clack*."
~ Rose Flannery, Founder of The Nourished Network

"*Navigating the Clickety-Clack* is an inspiring collection of tools and stories to nurture resilience and calm in the midst of life's chaos."
~Rebecca Whitecotton, Author of *Pull Your Self Together: A True Story of Alternate Realities, Spiritual Healing, and Dimensional Wholeness*

Contents

Acknowledgments

It with deep appreciation that I thank all the authors who said YES to participating in this powerful project.

Thanks to Bob Proctor, Jack Canfield, Christy Whitman, Marie Diamond, Adam Markel, Joe Vitale, Michael Beckwith, and John Demartini for being such great mentors and for always saying yes. Your support over the years has been instrumental in our success as authors and publishers.

Thank you to our incredible team who brought this book forward to completion and to the world one step at a time: Karen Burton, Heather Taylor, Bethany Knowles, Autumn Carlton, MaryDes, Rudy Milanovich, Viki Winterton, Pam Murphy, and Shannon Procise.

Thank you to all the teachers, speakers, and thought leaders who provided the tips, tools, and workshops that taught all the master teachers in this book how to stay peaceful, even during the Clickety-Clack of everyday life.

Introduction

Hello. My name is Keith Leon S., owner of Beyond Belief Publishing, and I want to welcome you to our book designed to help you in *Navigating the Clickety-Clack*. As we begin this journey together, you may not yet understand the title, but I am confident you navigate this troubling place from time to time. We all do.

Back in 2005, my wife, Maura, and I met a man named Fletch Rainey at the Agape International Center of Truth in California. We became good friends with Fletch. Eventually he created a group called "The Spiritual Posse" and became one of our spiritual mentors. We would reach out to him when we were freaking out about money, business challenges, fears, or when we were in flux, not knowing what to do next.

One time when we called him with one of our issues, he said, "Relax, you are just in the Clickety-Clack."

We asked, "What is the Clickety-Clack?"

Fletch said, "Remember when you had a ten-speed bicycle, and you changed from one gear to another? There is that moment when the chain is jumping from one gear to the next gear, but it has not clicked in yet. What sound does it make? *Clickety-clack . . . clickety-clack*. You have faith it will catch eventually, so you keep peddling the bike. Your faith pays off because it eventually catches, and when it does, you are off into an even better gear. That is where you are right now—you are in the Clickety-Clack. Have faith and know that things will kick in to the next gear soon enough. Trust, and know that all is well."

His reply would stay with us, and to this day, when Maura and I are experiencing worry or not knowing what to do next, one of us will look at the other and say, "Clickety-Clack." Other times I have experienced the Clickety-Clack are when others around me are freaking out, coming unglued, being judgmental, hateful, or angry toward me.

In a world filled with so much anger, resentment, judgment, hate, shame, and finger-pointing, how is one supposed to stay peaceful?

Over the years, I have developed tools to remain calm and peaceful in these times. People have asked me how I am able to do this. The answer is multi-layered, and it has taken me years to arrive at this point.

Here are some practices that have helped me over the years:

- Experiential growth workshops
- *The Work* of Byron Katie
- Prayer and meditation
- Teachings from the mystics
- Minding my thoughts and language

In the spring of 2020, the COVID-19 pandemic kept us all in our homes. This was a time of inner reflection for me. I took time to go within and look for answers to the question: *What's next for me?* I had visions of our dear friend Fletch and his teaching us about the Clickety-Clack. I thought: *If ever there were a time to stay calm and peaceful, it's now.*

With so much seemingly toxic information, news, and energy around us, wouldn't now be a great time to gain some tools for neutrality? I thought to myself: *I know people who are living these principles every day. I am friends with people who are able to stay peaceful, even now.* This thought led me to reach out to three dear friends and mentors, Bob Proctor, Jack Canfield, and Christy Whitman. I shared the title and subtitle with them, and they said they would love to participate in this book.

Next, I made a short list of other friends I knew who were walking and talking demonstrations of staying peaceful when others would not be able to do so. I contacted these friends and asked them if they would like to participate. At the end of each call, I asked each friend, "Do you know someone who is living a peace-filled life in a seemingly toxic world?" The people they recommended actually appear in these pages. It was important to me that every person in this book lives this principle.

Each person in this book is living what they will share and teach you!

I suggest taking your time reading this book. Read one story at a time, then stop and meditate on what was shared. Take notes, write in a journal, decide if there is a next step you would like to take, such as researching teachers, programs, or seminars recommended.

I have put together for you the finest group of people to share their Clickety-Clack stories, how they navigated out of the Clickety-Clack, and how they are able to stay peaceful inside, no matter what is happening outside. May you enjoy each and every word. May you be guided to next steps and ultimately discover what is called *the peace that passes all understanding.*

Michael Beckwith

How has the Clickety-Clack shown up in your life?

To me, the Clickety-Clack is moving from one paradigm to another for one of two reasons—or a combination of both. In the first situation, you expand your awareness of who you are, your personal sense of self. If you see yourself apart from God, creation, or Light, the Light riles up against this awareness and sends up hindrances to your next level of unfolding. A second situation may occur if there is a destruction or dissolution of your previous structures. Things seem to go haywire for a while, similar to the caterpillar breaking down to become the butterfly.

I see the Clickety-Clack as something that precedes the next level of unfolding quantumly. The *chaos theory*—in a layperson's terms—says that behind chaos there is an order trying to emerge. I have always taught that chaos precedes emergence.

Over these last couple of weeks, I did a seven-day intensive meditation training As I looked at the arc of my own life, this particular training took me back to before high school and showed me events leading up to the present moment. It showed me that every attack or seeming loss was followed by a boom, expansion of awareness, or tremendous blessing. I saw that different challenges and chaos were followed by an upliftment.

The guiding principle during these times of chaos was to stay out of worry, fretting, and anxiousness and to practice awareness.

I needed to be aware that:

1. All my needs are met.

2. Life is *for* me, and there is nothing against me.

3. If something wonderful is happening, it is trying to happen through me.

I try to stay in the framework of affirmative prayer in my sacred meditation time, in the progressive nature of the universe. Einstein asked the question: "Is the universe friendly?" I say not only is it friendly, it is progressive. It is always expanding, and we participate in it by staying in the dynamics I described above.

There have been many times in the development of Agape where there did not seem to be a way out of some issue, and then, things lifted to another level. When we first moved into the building at Buckingham, there came a moment there when we had to leave the old building. We did not yet have a new building. We were meeting at hotels. When we finally found the building that was appropriate for us, it needed a lot of work, and we went to the city council to get a conditional use permit for our spiritual community. It was not unanimous; a lot of people argued they did not want us in that building, but overwhelmingly, the city council and the mayor loved what Agape was all about and wanted us in their communities. We got the permission of use permit. However, the caveat was we had to complete the necessary work to bring everything up to code within a particular period of time or we would lose the conditional use permit.

At this particular time, I stated I did not want to let go of any staff members and that we were still going to meet on a regular basis at hotels until this building was prepared. We were burning through our cash, all of our reserves as we kept staff on and paid for the hotels every week. We were spending on the construction of what ultimately would become our sanctuary and office space. We were approaching the deadline, and we did not have enough money. It was a Clickety-Clack moment!

How did you navigate the Clickety-Clack?

I called a board meeting on a Saturday with the board of trustees and the contractor who was doing the work for us.

I said to them, "Is it possible for us to complete this task by the proposed date?" I was asking if we would have enough money to complete this task.

Some people were bemoaning our fate, "I don't know. This is very difficult."

I said, "Wait a minute, hold on. I am not asking you how we are going to do this. I am asking you: Is it possible?"

I asked around the circle, one by one: "Is it possible?"

Some people were complaining a little bit, saying, "I do not know if we can do this."

I repeated, "Is it possible?"

One by one I received a *yes*, including the contractor. Yes, it is possible. I said, "Do a spiritual practice with me for the next week. All I want you to do is stay in the possibility. Do not ask how we are going to raise this money, do not ask how we are going to pay our staff, do not ask how we are going to complete this project. Just stay in the possibility. That is all I want from you."

They agreed, we prayed, and they left. That was a Saturday. We had an application for a loan to complete the project. On Tuesday, the owner of that bank walked by the guy who had our file and said, "What are you working on?"

He said, "I am working on this loan package for Agape, but they do not have any collateral."

We were borrowing around $300,000—something along those lines. The owner said, "Is that Beckwith?"

The loan officer said yes.

The owner said, "Oh, give them the money. They don't have any collateral? Michael Beckwith? Give them the money; it will be okay."

By Tuesday, we had the money to complete the project. The contractor called and said "I was so moved by your board meeting, I have decided to double up. I am going to have two teams working to complete this, an evening team and a daytime team. I am going to pay for it out of my own pocket because I trust you guys will pay me."

Within a couple of days, we had not only the money, we had the crews to complete the job within the time frame. We celebrated the opening of Agape with our stage and office space, and ultimately, we had a bookstore and all of that.

That was a deep Clickety-Clack moment. There was no visible way to get what we needed, but because everyone held the field of possibility—and stayed in that field—something marvelous showed up. When you are in the Clickety-Clack, you have to stay out of fear and worry to the best of your ability. Hold the field of possibility for the next great emergence. Emergence is trying to happen.

What tools do you recommend for staying peaceful in a seemingly toxic world?

Feeling provides the healing. One of my teachers back in the seventies, Homer Johnson, used to say, "It don't mean a thing, if it don't have that feeling." Eventually, I would say *the feeling provides the healing*.

I encourage people to do a couple of things. First, I invite them to close their eyes, relax the body, and think about a moment in their life where all their needs were met and they were at peace. It does not matter whether they were a child or a teenager or a young adult or so-called *middle-aged*, whatever that is—or older.

Then, I ask them not only to reflect upon that moment, but to invite that moment to be the activity of their awareness. I invite individuals to be aware that they are recalibrating their nervous system around peace and around all needs being met—perhaps safety or well-being, whatever quality appears to be missing at that moment. I ask them to take a couple of breaths and hold every inhalation for a few seconds to amplify the feeling. Then exhale.

It is simple. You take a breath, you suspend the breath, you amplify the feeling, and then you release. You take another breath; you amplify that feeling. So you're actually walking in the awareness that your need is met, that you are at peace, and that you are safe. Carry that dynamic.

If you practice this technique, you become more in tune with your intuition so wisdom and guidance and direction flow through you in in a way you can understand. Generally, when there is anxiety or fear or worry—I call that *static*—that static is clouding up the line, preventing you from catching the wisdom, the inspiration, or the guidance.

God is not an on and off system. God is an *Is* system: God is. Wisdom is. Love is. Intelligence is. Is—not will be. With static on the line, you cannot hear it, you cannot feel it.

However, when you do this exercise, you are dissolving the static so you can hear the eternal broadcast:

> *Let there be Light.*
> *Let there be Life.*
> *Let there be Beauty.*
> *Let there be Intelligence.*
> *Let there be Abundance.*

You can hear it with your ears, but you see it with consciousness. Then, you are able to project it onto the screen of what some would call *the future*, which is really the extension of the now. The Spirit has gone before you to prepare a place because Spirit is everywhere.

When I have people do this, they can take their attention temporarily off the world of effects. For many people, peace and joy and harmony are a temporary respite against their fear. When things are going well in the world of effects, they are happy, and when things are not going well, they are sad.

This practice gives you a sense of peace not at all to the world of effects. It is your intrinsic nature. The world of effects then changes because it is condensed energy based on the quality of energy you are holding. It is a simple, yet profound, spiritual practice, you see.

About the Author

Michael Bernard Beckwith is the Founder and Spiritual Director of Agape International Spiritual Center in Los Angeles. Founded in 1986, Agape is a trans-denominational community comprised of thousands of local members and global live streamers. Highly regarded for its cultural, racial, and spiritual diversity and inclusivity, the late Coretta Scott King wrote to Dr. Beckwith, "I greatly admire what you are doing to bring about the Beloved Community, which is certainly what my dear husband worked for and ultimately gave his life." Widely recognized for his teachings on the science of inner transformation and unity, Dr. Beckwith embraces a practical approach to spirituality utilizing meditation, affirmative prayer, and Life Visioning™, a spiritual technology he developed for conscious evolution, authentic living, and living our life purpose. These practices teach us to take the experience of inner peace and awakened awareness into our everyday lives.

Dr. Beckwith is a sought-after meditation teacher, conference speaker, and seminar leader on the Life Visioning Process™.

He's addressed audiences at the UN General Assembly during its annual World Interfaith Harmony Week, TEDx Maui, and Oprah Winfrey Network's (OWN) *SuperSoul Sessions*, among numerous others. As cofounder and president of the Association for Global New Thought, he has hosted conferences featuring harbingers of world peace, including His Holiness the Dalai Lama, and had the distinguished honor of presenting to Nelson Mandela the Gandhi King Award.

Three of his books—*Life Visioning*, *Spiritual Liberation*, and *TranscenDance Expanded*—have received the prestigious Nautilus Award. His new app, Beckwith Inspires, features essential spiritual tools, technologies, and practices to help shift perceptions and transform lives. Dr. Beckwith has appeared on OWN's *SuperSoul Sunday* and *Help Desk; Dr. Oz; CNN; The Oprah Show; Larry King Live; Tavis Smiley;* and in his own PBS special, *The Answer Is You*. He is a member of Oprah's esteemed inaugural SuperSoul 100. His weekly Instagram Live series, *For A Time Such as This*, airs Wednesdays at 1:00 p.m. Pacific Time.

To learn more, go to: www.AgapeLive.com.

Dr. John Demartini

How has the Clickety-Clack shown up in your life?

When I was eighteen years old, I attempted to go back to school after being a high school dropout. I took a GED and miraculously, through guessing, passed. I left school when I was young because I was told by my first-grade teacher that I would never be able to read, write, or communicate effectively, that I would never amount to anything or go far in life.

After I took that test and passed, I tried to take a college class because I had earned a high school degree. In the first class I took, I scored a twenty-seven, but I needed a seventy-two to pass. When I saw that number, I was so humiliated and embarrassed that I ran to my car and cried. I drove home with teary eyes and curled in a fetal position underneath a Bible stand Mom had in the living room. I was really having a low moment. I could not see light at the end of the tunnel. I could not see my dream of overcoming my learning problems, learning how to read, and becoming a teacher.

My mom came home from shopping and saw me on the floor. After hearing what had happened, she said, "Son, whether you become a great teacher and travel the world like you dream, whether you return to Hawaii and ride great waves like you have done, or return to the streets and panhandle as a bum—which

27

you have also done—I want you to know that no matter what you do, your father and I are going to love you, no matter what."

My hand spontaneously made a fist of determination, and I saw the vision in my mind of becoming a teacher. I said to myself: *I am going to master reading, studying, and learning. I am going to master teaching, traveling, and philosophy; and I am going to do whatever it takes, travel whatever distance, and pay whatever price to spread my service of love across this planet. I am not going to let any human being on the face of the planet, not even myself, interfere now.*

I was phenomenally determined; there was no turning back. I got up and hugged my mom and went into my bedroom and got a dictionary—a Funk & Wagnalls dictionary, which I still have today. I started memorizing thirty words a day, and with the help of my mom, who tested me on spelling, pronunciation, and meaning of the thirty words a day, I grew my vocabulary enough to pass school.

Once I started passing, I did not stop, and I began to excel. Thankfully, this crisis yielded seeds of opportunities and blessings because of my mom's comment. If I had not had that comment, I do not know what would have happened. So I experienced the Clickety-Clack and could not see my dream and vision. I was so dispirited, I almost lost my vision, but it came back suddenly when someone cared about me.

My mom showed me *love* and *appreciation*, and she had *certainty* and *presence*. I call these the *four cardinal pillars of contribution and self-mastery.* She really made a difference in my life, my mom. Here I am, forty-eight and a half years later, still learning and teaching. So that was a Clickety-Clack moment turned into a momentum-building drive.

How did you navigate the Clickety-Clack?

When I ate, I sat with an encyclopedia and dictionary in front of me. I looked up every word I did not understand and practiced pronouncing it. I was determined to grow my vocabulary. By the end of that year, my vocabulary growth was accelerating. In reality, I often learned more than thirty words a day, but thirty words was the minimum.

My mom asked me right before my nineteenth birthday, "What do you want for you birthday, Son?"

I said, "I want the greatest teachings on the face on the Earth, the greatest writings by the greatest minds who ever lived. I want to be able to understand them."

She looked and paused. Finally, she said, "You sure you don't want a T-shirt?"

I said, "No, Mom. I want the greatest teachings on the face of the Earth. I want to stand on the shoulders of giants."

She had a brother, Ralph, who was a chemical physicist and once a professor at MIT. She must have called him on the phone because a couple of weeks later, right at my birthday, two giant six-by-six-foot wooden crates arrived on a flatbed truck at our house. After they unloaded them onto the ground, I got a crowbar out and opened these crates to find thousands of books. Thousands! I carried them inside and filled my room with books.

I read eighteen to twenty hours a day. If I was not at the house reading, I was reading on the way to school, in the library, or on the way back home. I wanted to catch up with all the other kids. Thanks to my mom, I wanted to do something exceptional. As my learning accelerated, students started asking me questions. Soon, the gatherings grew from one to two to a multitude of students who wanted to know what I was learning.

That experience was one of the most inspiring in my life: someone wanted to listen to me when I had been told I would never be able to read and write. My mom provided perseverance and opportunities, and they were the catalysts that led to where I am today.

What tools do you recommend for staying peaceful in a seemingly toxic world?

No matter what is happening in your life, ask yourself:

- *How is it helping me fulfill what I believe is my mission?*

- *How is it on the way and not in my way?*

- *What is it developing in me that I will require to fulfill my mission?*

- *What strength is it providing that will empower me?*

- *What leads or opportunities or context is it awakening?*

- *How is it helping me fulfill my mission, what is most deep, meaningful, and important in my life?*

Do not become a victim of history by saying: *I do not know.* Become a matter of destiny by not stopping until you find out the *how.* We have experiences we think are traumatic or terrible, but a day, a week, a month, a year, or five years later, we look back, and we say *thank you.* So why wait for the wisdom of the ages that comes with the aging process when you can have that wisdom by asking right now: *How is it helping me fulfill my mission?*

Next, ask yourself: *What is the highest priority action I can do right now to help fulfill my mission?* Take command and prioritize your action steps and perceptions, understanding that, no matter what happens, your self-worth and potential will expand. You will magnetize the people, places, things, ideas, and events that will synchronize with that intention in order to achieve something momentum building and impactful.

About the Author

Dr. John Demartini is a world-renowned specialist in human behavior, a researcher, author, and global educator. He was recently selected as Top Human Behavior Specialist of the Year for 2020 by the IAOTP for his outstanding leadership and commitment to the profession.

Dr. John Demartini is the founder of the global education organization, the Demartini Institute, which has over seventy-two courses on self-development, life mastery, and leadership in its extensive curriculum. Dr. Demartini's knowledge is the culmination of over forty-eight years of cross-disciplinary research. As an educator, he travels full time around the world, addressing both public and professional audiences in media, talks, seminars, and consultations in which he teaches people self-governance and how to develop their leadership and empowerment in all areas of their lives.

Dr. Demartini is a dynamic, results-driven leader who has demonstrated success not only as one of the world's leading human behavioral specialists, but also as an Executive Coach who has studied over 30,000 books across all the defined academic disciplines and has synthesized the wisdom of the ages which he shares on stage in over one hundred countries.

Dr. Demartini is the author of over forty self-development books including the best-seller *The Breakthrough Experience* and his new global release, *The Values Factor*. He has produced an extensive library of CDs and DVDs that cover topics ranging from financial mastery to business mastery, relationship development to health and healing, the art of communication to inspiring education and leadership. He has been featured in film documentaries such as *The Secret*, *The Opus*, and *Oh My God*, alongside Ringo Starr, Seal, and Hugh Jackman. He has shared the stage with some of the world's most influential speakers, such as Stephen Covey, Sir Richard Branson, Wayne Dyer, Deepak Chopra, and Donald Trump; and been interviewed on the world's leading television and radio networks, such as *Larry King Live*, *The Early Show*, and *Wall Street*; and magazine publications, such as *Shape*, *Leadership*, *Success*, *Prestige*, *Entrepreneur*, and *O* (Oprah).

Connect with Dr. Demartini via his website: DrDemartini.com

On Facebook: facebook.com/drjohndemartini

On LinkedIn: linkedin.com/in/drjohndemartini

On YouTube: youtube.com/drdemartini

On Instagram: instagram.com/drjohndemartini/

Christina Frazier

How has the Clickety-Clack shown up in your life?

It was the spring of 2016. My business partner pulled the wool over my eyes and claimed my business for herself. The business was my brainchild; I was the sole visionary and sole creator. The experience brought me to my knees.

How did you navigate the Clickety-Clack?

I gathered myself in ways a warrior gathers herself after a battle—*I dug in*. I could see an armor being put on me. I went to my spiritual toolbox of twenty-five-plus years and gathered all my most profound teachers, lessons, and aha moments. Then, I meditated. And I meditated some more. I meditated in my space that my clients often refer to as *healing and cozy*—rich with colors, textures, and fresh flowers—a space that envelopes the five senses.

Creating a beautiful intentional space helped me heal. I meditated throughout the day for weeks on end, and I listened to what my wisdom body had to say. My intuition was guiding me thoroughly. I gathered purposefully with my best friends who were outrageously funny—those who could make me laugh. My mother always used to say, "Laughter is the best medicine!"

I raised my level of self-care to a new height and only gravitated toward the things that made me feel good and brought me joy. I received massages, energy work, and intuitive readings; found support in nature; gathered with my closest friends; and took healing baths rich in salts, botanicals, and essential oils. By allowing myself to be in the gifts of imperfection, somehow everything was perfect as it was. Something new was unfolding, and I was experimenting on new ways to navigate this crisis. In hindsight, the offerings I was receiving were *rich*.

I created a Vision board that said:

HAVE THE COURAGE TO DREAM BIGGER

and

YOU ARE A BAD ASS

I practiced prayer, ritual, mantras, and surrender. These practices were most profound to me!

During my meditation, I said, "Show me the highest and the best way I can be in the world!"

I let go fully of everything. I went to a place I had never experienced before on my own. I. Let. Go. I experienced what I refer to as *spiritual warrior boot camp*. And yes, it changed me forever.

What tools do you recommend for staying peaceful in a seemingly toxic world?

One of my most influential teachers, Russell Delman, *The Embodied Life*, helped shift and shape me in into the most luminous being. I had the pleasure of taking a three-and-a-half-year mentorship program of his work and its three main components: Embodied Meditation, Feldenkrais movement lessons, and Guided Inquiry. All are based on bringing *presence* and *curiosity* to the present moment.

Here is a powerful practice he calls Ground-Sound-Breath. This practice is so simple yet most powerful—an immensely helpful stress-reducing technique that takes only minutes to do.

Ground

Find a quiet place and sit comfortably. Remove your shoes. Be still and close your eyes. Feel the place where you are sitting: Sense your bottom on the chair; sense the cushion or fabric on your bottom. Just notice. Feel your feet on the ground. You can also lie down and feel the surface supporting you.

Sound

Become aware of sounds around you. Allow the sounds to move through you and around you, like clouds passing across the sky. All you need to do is notice the sounds coming and going. It's that simple.

Breathe

Follow your breathing for three consecutive cycles. Allow your belly and lungs to rise and fall. Notice the air coming through your nose. Let the sound and ground drift away as you are breathing. Just breathe.

TA-DA! That's it. Take a moment to notice how you feel. You may experience calmness, shifts in mood, less muscular pain, or a shift in attitude.

Another practice for experiencing peace is *Ritual.* Ritual to me is intention, a recipe to living a harmonious life. The key is turning routine into ritual.

How do you live?

The first step in this practice is to notice how you approach what you are doing. Don't just pull the honey jar from the cupboard. Instead, feel the texture of the jar, feel the sweetness touching your tongue, and appreciate the bees that make it and the supporting family farm who sells it.

I absolutely love self-care rituals—dry brushing before my bath, lighting candles—these are daily rituals as well. Some specific rituals might be: a money magnet ritual, love rituals, or family rituals during the Christmas season. I created a business, Adirondack Foot Sanctuary, where clients experience foot treatments infused with ritual. This combination creates a unique blend for healing and inner guidance. I've developed and proven this concept.

Tools such as gemstones, flower essences, mudras, mantras, healing music, and smudging all set the scene for transformation and will help you navigate the Clickety-Clack. Ritual allows you to connect on deeper level and appreciate the beauty of the sensory-rich journey of your everyday living.

These little rituals are basically the same because they connect us to our higher self and our true essence. Calm. Reset. Recalibrate. We are starved for all three. I hope *the ritual way of thinking* will encourage you to delve more deeply into your life so you may discover ways to live up to your highest potential.

About the Author

Originally from upstate New York, Christina Frazier lived in Bend, Oregon, for thirty years before returning to her beloved Adirondack Mountains where she lives with her partner, Mark, and her kitty named Cash. Christina has over twenty-five years' experience in the spa and wellness industry. She taught for ten years within the Massage Therapy Program at Central Oregon Community College. There, she founded the Spa Training curriculum. She has also worked as a trainer for Sundari, an Ayurvedic international-inspired product line, teaching Ayurvedic principles and Sundari facials, body treatments, and massage.

Frazier's travels have brought her through the United States, Asia, and Europe, allowing her to experience world class and premier spas, private tours, and teachings from influencers in Asian and European philosophies involving hydrotherapy, products, treatments, and massage. As a visionary and entrepreneur, she has the ability to create healing spaces and ritual practices. She holds the title and licensure of Massage Therapist, Reiki Master, Educator, and Spa Consultant. She combines a mixture of compassionate presence, humor, and kindness into her work.

Christina believes in the art of relaxation, is inspired by beauty, and loves to travel.

You may contact Christina at:

Email: Christina@adkfootsanctuary.com

Website: www.adirondackfootsanctuary.com

Lianne Hofer

How has the Clickety-Clack shown up in your life?

The Clickety-Clack has shown up a number of times in my life. The one I would like to share—the one that was the most transformational—was the one that showed up about ten years ago. My husband and I were living in New Jersey and decided we did not want to stay there any longer.

We started looking at where we wanted to go, and we couldn't come up with anything, so we decided to *trust*. In his business, my husband was offered an opportunity to go to North Carolina for a new sales territory. When he got the news, he called me that afternoon and said, "Start packing; we are moving."

We moved to a state where we did not know anyone; we moved to a city where we did not know anyone. Everything was different. We had a young child in grammar school. I left my career of twenty-five years. North Carolina was one of the states that did not have reciprocity with any of the states I was licensed in as a dental hygienist.

Shortly after moving, we were digging into savings as we were without my income and my career money, and my husband received a pay cut. We were overwhelmed, and I spent my time sitting on the sofa playing app games on my phone, having no sense of purpose in life.

I looked at my husband and said, "There has got to be more than this. I have way too much energy to do this."

How did you navigate the Clickety-Clack?

I realized I was feeling completely overwhelmed and out of control, so I took a break, caught my breath, and asked myself what I could I do—what were the tools I could use. I was a dental hygienist, and I took sixty copies of my resume out to local dentists and handed them out. That generated no phone calls. Not a one.

A neighbor of ours was a sales rep in the dental industry, and he knew a lot of dentists. He asked around, and that generated no calls. I would have been happy to just sit at a desk and answer a phone or file or clean rooms. It did not matter; I needed something to do. Nothing came back.

My husband and I sat there and looked at each other. He said, "Well, you are not supposed to do that anymore. Now what are you going to do?"

We bought an airline ticket, and I went back to New Jersey to hang out with some girlfriends and spend some time with family. One night at ten o'clock, I was sitting on my girlfriend's sofa. We had a couple of glasses of wine, and we needed a snack. I went over to the pantry and stuck my hand in a bag. As I tasted the snack, I said, "Throw this away; it is stale."

She looked at me and said, "Oh my god, that is what you need to do."

I think: *Eat stale snacks? What am I supposed to do?*

She said, "You always come over here and organize my junk drawer and clean out my pantry. That is what you need to do."

I investigated what it was like to own a small business because I had worked for a small business owner as a hygienist. I ended up creating a business called The Clutter Consultant, which is still going strong ten years later and has supported my family.

I came back to North Carolina, where, fortunately, there were not a lot of organizers at the time—there you go. It was scary as hell. It felt like standing at the edge of a cliff and looking down at the Grand Canyon with a bungee cord on. Even though I knew it was okay to jump, it was scary as hell. I couldn't help myself. I had to do it.

It is the best thing I ever did.

What tools do you recommend for staying peaceful in a seemingly toxic world?

The first overarching tool I recommend is positivity. Try to maintain as much positivity as you can, even when it is hard. Control what you consume because you are what you consume.

Some suggestions to encourage positivity:

1. Watch the inner talk. How do you talk to yourself? Do you talk to yourself like your best friend, or do you talk to yourself like you are not your best friend?

2. Surround yourself with people who have great mindsets, especially when they are talking to you. If you don't have that ability, surround yourself with quotes from thought leaders like Albert Einstein or Rumi.

3. Listen to things on YouTube. I do not listen to the radio anymore. I listen to Abraham; I listen to Hindu music chants; I listen to positive things.

The second tool is to treat everybody the way you want to be treated. Before I get out of the car to talk to a client, I say to myself: *Allow me to be a blessing today. How can I be a blessing? How can I serve this person?*

The third tool is to ditch the judgment—judgment of yourself and judgment of people around you—because everybody does the best they can in each moment. Remember, your best and their best right now may be different in ten minutes or in ten hours. Try to meet people where they are. I hope these tools help you craft a peaceful and rewarding life.

About the Author

Lianne Hofer created The Clutter Consultant to help her family finances while doing something she loved: organizing. Along the way, massive personal and spiritual growth occurred in her life. Her confidence grew, triggering speaking engagements for trainings, live audiences, podcasts, radio, and television programs. Believing that what we are searching for is under our clutter, she inspires the joy that decluttering reveals. National publications, books, and local articles have featured her wisdom.

Lianne served in business leadership roles for eWomen and BNI, and as a Reiki Master/Master Teacher, she co-founded the Charlotte Reiki Clinic for children and teens in North Carolina. Certified with Marci Shimoff, as a *Happy for No Reason* trainer, she brings positive, happy energy while infusing interactions with universal love.

Through serving her clients, Liane strides toward her ultimate purpose of inspiring happiness, generating optimism, and living with a lot less *stuff.*

Find Lianne on
Facebook at facebook.com/TheClutterConsultant
or connect through her website at LianneHofer.com.
To claim a free gift, visit: LianneHoferAuthor.com/Clickety-Clack.

Inge Jechart

How has the Clickety-Clack shown up in your life?

The Clickety-Clack has shown up a couple of times for me. The last time it happened was about eleven years ago, when I faced an unexpected divorce. After I found out that we were going to divorce, I woke up every morning thinking: *This is not happening to me.* But it was.

It was a long, drawn-out process, and it was very difficult. By then, I had been doing some of my own emotional growth work for about five years, and that really helped. However, my life still felt as if it had become untethered. Because quitting my job had felt overdue for a long time, I went ahead with that too.

I had a high schooler and an older kid at home, and both were going through some rough times. I was basically a single parent at that time, and I did not know what I wanted to do next professionally. For many years, I had been a project manager in the tech industry, but I did not want to continue in that field.

I had this feeling of floating in space with no mooring, a feeling of uncertainty. That was my Clickety-Clack situation.

How did you navigate the Clickety-Clack?

I navigated the Clickety-Clack by leaning heavily on my community of friends and coaches. I doubled down on the emotional growth work I had been doing. I secured coaching for myself, including an expensive weekend intensive, but I was willing to invest in myself.

I also slowed down my life a lot. I took time to learn, to investigate, to research, and to study. I attended many self-development workshops, including Byron Katie's *School for the Work*. Then, I earned a two-hundred-hour yoga teaching certificate, which took a year to complete. That intensive program was the best thing I had ever done for my body, and, as a bonus benefit, I made a number of good friends.

I also had many deep discussions with friends about life, how to show up in life, and how to be a good person. The work with my coaches focused on my need for unconditional love to be happy and live a good life. I took time for myself to grow my inner strength, my capacities, and my circle of trusted friends. My overwhelming feeling was that my life had gone from living in two dimensions to living in three dimensions.

What tools do you recommend for staying peaceful in a seemingly toxic world?

These tools really supported me during my journey and continue to support me now:

First, I found a community where I could be myself, where I could openly share, not be judged, and be accepted for who I was and for who I am. In fact, over the last few years, I have helped create such a community, and it is available to everyone. We even have free group-coaching calls twice a week that are open to anyone. The URL is UnconditionallyLoving.com. A loving community is really the most important tool.

Second, finding support and coaching from people who can love and see me, who have wisdom, and who are just a few steps ahead of me emotionally has been vital for me.

Third, I try to meditate several times a week. Sitting in meditation might not work for everybody, but it works well for me. You may want to try a different form of meditation, but the idea is basically to spend some time being still, to help calm the loud thoughts in your mind.

Last, but not least, it is important for me to move my body. I have never in my life called this *exercise* because that sounds like a lot of work. Instead, I do what feels like fun, and I have been doing that since I was twenty years old. I have never stopped because I don't want to.

About the Author

Inge Jechart, PhD, is a certified Relationship and Parenting Coach. For more than ten years, Inge has worked with her clients to help them vitalize and enjoy their relationships, and to lead happy, productive, and fulfilling lives.

Inge coaches individuals and couples throughout the United States and around the world. In addition to one-on-one coaching, she hosts relationship workshops, teaches parenting classes, and facilitates group coaching sessions.

Her work with parents has been informed by her own parenting struggles and the lessons she learned from these experiences. Frequently helping individuals and families navigate crises of divorce, addiction, and familial alienation, Inge guides parents and children to reconnect deeply, rooted in patience, kindness, healthy limits, and unconditional love.

Inge cares deeply; listens with a compassionate, open heart; and uses her finely tuned intuition to help her clients find different perspectives on life and to discover ways to experience the contentment and unconditional love they've been looking for.

To learn more and connect with Inge, visit:

Website: JechartCoaching.com for a free coaching consultation

FaceBook: facebook.com/jechartcoaching

Instagram: @coach_inge

Erin Kinney

How has the Clickety-Clack shown up in your life?

The Clickety-Clack has shown up in my life a lot in the past two years. In 2019, my marriage ended, and my world completely fell apart. I shared a business and its location space with my ex-husband. He moved out of the house, and I was moving out of my business location. I was frantically trying to set up a new office while treating all my patients and taking care of my kids.

There was a lot going on. It was a crunchy part of that Clickety-Clack. There were times I did not think I was going to make it through a particular day. Then about five or six months later, the world shut down because of the pandemic, and I quickly had to re-think life as we knew it, with childcare, homeschooling, and running a business that now needed to be conducted online.

I take care of a lot of patients, so there was a lot of Clickety-Clack. For the next year, I was dealing with divorce and taking care of many patients who were really struggling while I was also struggling. I specialize in treating anxiety and depression, particularly for women in high-stress situations.

Not only was I dealing with a high patient volume, but my practice grew about 300 percent during the COVID year. I had a huge increase in business—which I am extremely grateful for—and it was wonderful, but it also meant a lot more Clickety-Clack in my life. There were a lot more moving pieces.

I was also homeschooling one of my children at the same time. I had several employees, and my business continued to grow.

How did you navigate the Clickety-Clack?

I navigated the Clickety-Clack by taking my life one day at a time. There were some days I had to take one hour at a time. I was in many different caretaking roles with my children, my family, my patients, and my employees. In order to show up as my best self, I needed to function at a seven out of ten—at least—and, honestly, there were some days I was not close to that.

The process that kept me grounded was prayer. I hadn't prayed in a long while but had become good at practicing meditation. I had always been good at practicing meditation. At some point during the pandemic year, one of my patients was talking about her own journey, and she shared her distinction between prayer and meditation.

She said, "Prayer is the asking, and meditation is the listening."

For a long time, I had been listening a lot, but I had not actually been asking for the help I needed. So, during the time when the Clickety-Clack was really in my life, I started asking, and I returned to prayer. I said, *Hey, I need to find this person who will help me in this part of my business, or I need to find this nanny.*

I prayed specifically about what I needed, and I also continued my meditation practice. The answers to my prayers would sometimes show up in meditation. Other times, they would show up literally at my door or I would receive a Facebook message or an Instagram DM. In short, the answers came in many forms.

The biggest piece in navigating the Clickety-Clack was learning to ask for what I needed so I could show up as my best self.

What tools do you recommend for staying peaceful in a seemingly toxic world?

I have been recommending these tools for a long time, but I think I did not know how powerful they were until I was in the Clickety-Clack. I always knew the tools I recommended worked, but when I started using them myself, I had proof they work.

First is the asking piece, **prayer**. Ask for what you need. If you do not ask for what you need, it may or may not show up. But if you ask, it is *always* going to show up. Ask for what you need in a relationship, in a job, with your children, or in a relationship with a higher power. Prayer is the best form of asking for what you need.

The second part is **meditation**, the listening aspect. Spend at least five minutes in meditation a day as the listening piece. You need to spend quiet time every day to listen for what is going to show up.

My third tip I recommend to many of my patients: take ten minutes a day, preferably in the afternoon, to lie flat and close your eyes. I call this **getting horizontal**. I have found this practice life-changing for a lot of my patients and for myself. I try to lie down for ten minutes every day. Sometimes I will read, sometimes I will listen to something, and sometimes I will meditate. It is a little time-out or recharge time.

When you lie flat:

- It calms your nervous system

- It moves you out of fight-or-flight mode.

- Your blood pressure goes down.

- Your heart rate decreases.

- It allows you to come back to yourself.

A lot of people have a hard time navigating the Clickety-Clack or navigating this toxic world when they are not at their best self. If you allow yourself to come back to who you truly are, the world becomes a lot easier to navigate.

To recap: prayer, meditation, and getting horizontal—those are my three tips.

About the Author

Dr. Kinney is a Naturopathic doctor, speaker, author, and podcast host who helps stressed-out patients improve their mood, balance their hormones, and increase their energy. She is incredibly passionate about teaching her patients to understand why stress causes so many problems in the body and how they can change their response to stress so they can take back control in both their bodies and their lives. She received a bachelor of arts from Vanderbilt University and was a summa cum laude graduate of the University of Bridgeport College of Naturopathic Medicine (UBCNM).

She currently runs a private practice in Annapolis, Maryland, where she specializes in treating patients with chronic health conditions related to hormonal and nervous system imbalances. In addition to her practice, she offers workshops, retreats, and online programs. When not practicing medicine, you can find her reading, doing yoga, spreading awareness about Naturopathic medicine, or spending time with her two young daughters.

If you want to learn more about Dr. Kinney's methods, go to her website www.drerinkinney.com and grab her free Ultimate Stress Reset Webinar or follow her on Instagram @drkinney to watch videos and learn more about her offerings!

Julianna Jaffe Leven

How has the Clickety-Clack shown up in your life?

When I reread the definition of the Clickety-Clack, I realized I lived there from the time I entered junior high until I was thirty-four years old.

I was a happy, loving little girl who loved to love everybody. Then, I hit junior high, and my world changed. There wasn't much space for loving as far as I could see—for myself or others. Like so many of us, I tried. Oh, God! How I tried. I tried to be the son my father never had. I tried to be like the other girls, but I simply didn't care about what they cared about.

My Clickety-Clack was spent searching, trying on different things. I went to three different universities in my four years of undergraduate education. I lived in England. I rejected Judaism. I entered the corporate world to great external success. I became the national sales manager for the entire automotive industry for a large data communications company.

And, I had to take two Excedrin I kept on my nightstand and wait 15 minutes before I could start my day without a pounding headache.

The Clickety-Clack stopped when I was sitting in my therapist's office after having had an extreme panic attack at an industry and trade show. He turned to me and said, "If you could be doing anything in the world you wanted to do, and money was not an issue, what would you be doing?"

The words fell out of my mouth without any conscious awareness, "I'd be sitting in your chair."

Four months later, I was in graduate school in a clinical program for a master's of science in Clinical Humanistic Psychology, and I swear—for the first time since I was eleven years old—I felt congruent with myself. I was home.

How did you navigate the Clickety-Clack?

I set a pattern in place back then; I navigated the Clickety-Clack by being relentless and never giving up. Even with all the *noise* I had going on, I always knew that life wasn't meant to be so painful, and that there was a better way to live.

I began searching for and finding teachers in earnest. Therapist after therapist. Then spiritual teachers. Some of them I met through books, some in person. Some were false; some were true. The false ones created an extreme Clickety-Clack. In one case, for years! Boy, did I learn a lot in those instances.

Learning what we don't want and what does not resonate with our truth can produce some powerful, deep *knowings*. Most importantly, I learned I have a voice inside that always tells me the truth. I became determined to learn more and more about that voice that I now know is my intuitive voice. This voice lives in the center of my heart; it *is* love and connects me to the Divine. When I follow that voice, I am always taken to a place of truth, a place of growth.

And the journey continues. Every time the Clickety-Clack gets noisy, I realize *there's change a-coming*. Over time, the Clickety-Clack has become a clearer and clearer messenger, telling me that it's time for the next shift. When it appears in my life, I know I am being called to step into the next level. Once, I thought I would die if I went there, and to this day, a part of me does die. However, it's always a part of me I need to let go of to find more freedom, more growth, more joy, and more happiness.

What tools do you recommend for staying peaceful in a seemingly toxic world?

First and foremost, above all else: **Know that you are love**. There is nothing else that is real. I know that sounds cliché and too easy. It is not complex, yet it is true and challenges the bejeebers out of us.

We need help. We all need help. We are not designed to be solitary beings. We need one another. We have big, big blind spots. It is nearly impossible for us to see what is getting in the way of living our beautiful selves without *mirrors* in the form of teachers, guides, and a community to reflect our truth back to us.

Ask for help and **don't give your power away**. Remember everyone you are talking to is human also. They have blind spots. They have flaws. I love this saying: *Only trust what is said to you by others if it agrees with your own reason and resonates with your heart.* We each know our own truth in our hearts, and others help us remember and reconnect with our deepest truths.

With the help of my truest teacher and mentor, Dr. Paul Dugliss, I moved from psychotherapy to transformational life coaching and spiritual mentoring. I found that our deepest growth and our hopes for a life of fulfillment, peace, and happiness all require we go beyond the minds and emotions.

It was with Dr. Dugliss that I discovered the beautiful tool of Heart-based Meditation. After a lot of kicking and screaming, I have fallen in love with this tool. So much so, I have become a Heart-based Meditation instructor. It is a key component in my work with clients, as I have the honor to be a *sherpa* (coach) with people on their journey to awakening their hearts—falling in love with themselves and leading happier, more joy-filled, and more meaningful lives.

About the Author

In addition to her formal education at both the University of Michigan as an undergrad and the Center for Humanistic Studies for graduate work, Julianna Jaffe Leven brings to her clients the wisdom, knowledge, and gifts of one who has and continues to authentically *walk her own journey*. She has learned that guides, mentors, therapists, and coaches can only take their clients as far as they themselves have traveled.

One of her unique gifts is the ability to create a safe environment for people to unfold unto themselves, creating a safe space without judgment. Within that space, her clients gain clearer vision of what has been blocking their natural evolution into the fullest, most expressed version of themselves.

Leven loves speaking to groups about all aspects of *the journey*. Introducing individuals and groups to the gift of Heart-based Meditation is central to her practice, as she helps others utilize this powerful tool to lift themselves out of the *struggle* and into a space that affords ease and grace. She passionately carries forth the message: *It doesn't have to be so hard. Truly!*

To explore and learn more about this wondrous journey, she can be reached at Awakening Heart Transformational Life Coaching and Spiritual Mentoring:

By phone: 248-514-4542

By email: julianna@awakeningheartcoaching.com

Mike Mantic

How has the Clickety-Clack shown up in your life?

About three and a half years ago, I was working for company in Australia, a small eight-figure company. The job was great for my experience, but it was a toxic environment. Over the time I worked there, I became more and more stressed and felt more and more trapped. It was a real estate investing education company, and I got caught up in the marketing I was helping create.

I started to lose all sense of myself; I did not have any vision for my own future. I was getting up every morning and dragging myself to work. My body was in pain. I was not sleeping properly. It was a toxic environment, and I knew I had to move on. I knew I had to do something, but I did not know what it was.

I had absolutely no vision of my future. I lost all sense of who I was or what was motivating me. I found myself in the Clickety-Clack, knowing I had to move on but not knowing what to do or how to do it, I knew I had to transform that *stuck* feeling into a new vision of what I wanted to create in my life. This is when it all started to turn around.

How did you navigate the Clickety-Clack?

First, I meditated on how I wanted my day to be. I asked myself what I wanted each day to look like and how I wanted to spend my time. It was important for me to *feel* the difference between where I was and where I wanted to go. I wanted to design my life so that I could feel joy.

Second, I connected with a soul-level intuitive source where I discovered what I wanted to create in this life. When I incarnated into this body, I came here with a mission to experience and to create certain things. I tuned in to that soul-level message of what I wanted *before* I incarnated and went through the process of forgetting that part of the incarnation process. We come into our physical body, and we forget our connection to our soul as part of the incarnation process. I connected to that soul-level journey.

Third, I intuitively connected to the obvious next steps. I knew what I wanted to create and what I wanted my daily experience to be. I intuitively connected every single day to what was obvious—the next thing I should do to create these experiences in my life. What was *intuitively* obvious was not necessarily logically obvious, and finding what was intuitively obvious gave me my next steps. Then, I acted on those intuitive messages.

I followed those intuitive instructions over three or four months, and I completely replaced my income. I quit that job. I started working from home and living the life I had designed on a day-to-day basis—going for walks, writing, and working for myself and others. That is how I managed to get out of that situation.

What tools do you recommend for staying peaceful in a seemingly toxic world?

The **first tool** is realizing we each have an egoic identity, and that egoic identity is archaically hardwired to focus on fear and survival. That is what it is designed to do. But we also have this other side of us, a *soul-creator* self, that is focused on love and creativity. It is up to us to decide where we place our attention.

Most people—and certainly this was true of me at the time—have no idea they are focused on fear and survival. Often, it seems like they are doing the logical thing, but they are focused on what they fear. If you do not know how to differentiate between low-level information from your ego versus higher quality information from your intuition, you will end up creating the opposite of what you want. Telling the difference is a learned skill.

The **second tool** is envisioning what your heart and soul would love to create, regardless of any negative circumstances that seem to hold power. Then, step daily into that space where you are connected to the creative self, identifying yourself as a creator and a soul. You must deliberately choose what your soul wants to create over your egoic survival creations. You do this by connecting daily to the vision of the soul-informed end result you are choosing to create.

The **third tool** is taking action on those steps you intuitively receive. Look for the obvious based on what is in your heart and what you would love to create. The obvious steps will come. You must take those steps, even if they are scary, even if you feel resistance. If you do not act on what you intuitively receive, then you may as well have not received that information. Taking action is part of receiving higher wisdom. I want to reiterate the importance of that: if you spend time getting intuitive, high-quality information, it still means nothing if you do not turn it into solid form. You do that by acting on the steps you intuitively receive. Then, you are actually able to receive what you desire.

About the Author

After a near-death experience at thirteen, Mike began a thirty-six-year journey of exploration in meditation, breath and body work, shamanism, alchemy, and altered states of consciousness. Mike's work comes from his soul mission and connects people to their soul-level intuition and highest wisdom in practical and creative ways.

Mike's mission is to help others explore the magical and multidimensional nature of the world and themselves from a place of accelerated awareness and expanded consciousness that allows them to deliberately co-create with their highest nature.

His explorations include preparing for death and maintaining a connection with dying people after they have passed. He also has explored precision intuition and trance work to help others tap into high-level creativity and express their most exciting and creative potential.

Discover why lists of your skills or *likes* may not lead you to discovering your true soul purpose. Let Mike take you on a five-day journey to explore your true nature and purpose, your soul's mission, and what your heart truly wants to create in this lifetime. Visit: www.synergism.co/ncc to gain access to a five-day guided trance and consciousness experience that could completely change the way you see the word, yourself, and your soul's mission. Usually $197, it's yours **free**.

Annabelle Merriman

How has the Clickety-Clack shown up in your life?

The Clickety-Clack happened as I went through challenges over the course of my life. Many times, I was not able to stop my downward spiral until I reached rock bottom. This happened a few times during my life as my body felt broken down, my mind shut down, and I felt numb and lost to the point of being locked down. I realized I needed to do something different, something better, because I could no longer let myself become so low, so desperate, so fearful, and so totally incapable of living life and doing what I was meant to do.

Ten years ago, after having breast cancer—a terrible experience—I had to change and face the Clickety-Clack in my life. I had to step up and take full responsibility for what was happening to me.

How did you navigate the Clickety-Clack?

I navigated by making a commitment to myself, making the decision not to stay at rock bottom. I became resourceful as I opened myself to receiving help. I wanted something different, and my intention was strong. One day, while walking in the neighborhood aimlessly, I said to myself: *This has to stop. There is more to life; I am not letting it pass by.*

I decided to commit to my soul calling and trust in the journey to find my true self. I realized I needed to give myself what I was craving from others—to feel valued and worthy. I brought new people into my life, and I started to educate myself. That was the start of my self-realization journey. I began to listen to my intuition and do things I felt were good for me. I refused to give up and give in easily to challenges, and I developed resilience and courage. Not giving up was a huge one, and to help, I followed the cycle of the moon as the dark and bright phases matched my cycles of up and down.

I chose to educate myself at all levels and to change my experience within, living life to meet myself and to learn *of* myself at a much deeper level. Knowing who I was, what I wanted, and what I was dreaming. For many years, I was focused on my family, being a wife, and bringing up my son—my priority at the time. When my son finished school, I realized I didn't have another dream for my life.

When I first started this journey, I did not know who I was. I lost my sense of identity—who I was—and I lost my passion for life. I was influenced by the culture of the outside world and was the victim of marketing and the spread of junk by the media. I had not connected to my deeper self, and I knew this was my big existential crisis. I had to find who I was after being a mother, a wife, and a health practitioner for so many years. The commitment to my inner call was the biggest change, to value myself and start the transformation work.

What tools do you recommend for staying peaceful in a seemingly toxic world?

First, I had to commit to letting go of what didn't serve me and to replacing it with love for myself. When I understood that I was the most important person in my life, I made time for myself and created daily rituals to nourish my body, mind, soul, and spirit. I connected to my deeper self through movement with soccer, yoga, dance, walking in nature, even shaking my body to move the energy that had kept me stuck. I moved stuck energy with breathing and singing, which was so liberating. I started to dance freely, sing often, and breathe deeply.

Having awareness of the emotional body and feeling my own body fully—with the highs and the lows—was a life changer. I accepted and fully loved my feeling body. I let my emotions come up and then let them go, not holding on to old suffering. Letting go is the master key.

Practicing anything that brings joy is ideal, as is finding the joy in every moment.

When working with the mind, I listened to inspiring leaders. I journaled daily with a strong focus on bringing gratitude at all times, setting intentions without being attached to the result, and learning new ways to understand my soul calling. There are lots of different facets of the self.

I used:

- The Human Design System, based on the teachings of Ra Uru Hu

- Astrology

- Gene Keys, based on the teachings of Richard Rudd

- The Expanded Love Method, from Kate Harlow, who helped me rebirth as Annabelle in 2019

These are amazing systems. I used EMDR (eye movement desensitization and reprocessing) for trauma healing, and many easy tools to relax my nervous system: mindfulness, meditation, contemplation, and grounding by walking in nature.

Finally, I connected to my spiritual self. Earlier in my life, I totally detached from spirituality because I associated it only with religion. In the last few years, I have opened myself to bring magic and miracles into my life by praying and believing in the heavens—with faith and trust in life again. The key is to be able to let go of control and fear by connecting with the heart.

Know yourself well and move from living a life of lack and victimhood in your shadow to manifesting your dreams. Master the self and shift your energy to manifest a new reality by changing your daily habits, thoughts, and beliefs. In this process, you can find your gift and bring magic and miracles to your life.

This process is confronting and liberating at the same time, which is why it is important to be guided by a professional. I valued myself enough to work with amazing mentors. I invested a lot of money for courses and retreats to help me through the changes. They guided me as I let go of the fear and embraced love and abundance to take life-changing decisions, making the impossible, possible.

I now guide my clients through the storms of life with love, compassion, and dedication. I educate, inspire, and empower women to reclaim their feminine power to manifest their ideal life.

Please accept these words from me as a gift for your journey.

In this unsteady world
I choose Love
For a pleasant future
I choose Love
For a peaceful life
I choose Love
To heal from the past
I choose Love
To nourish my soul
I choose Love
To fill my heart
I choose Love
Love is the only way

About the Author

Annabelle Merriman is a bestselling author and a Life Expansion Expert. She helps courageous female entrepreneurs reclaim their feminine inner power, without doubt or second guessing, so they can expand their possibilities and design life on their terms.

Annabelle's mission is to transform global anxiety about the future into unshakable trust and inner knowing, so women can all be guided by their inner voice to make grounded, wise, and powerful choices.

When women are empowered and guided by their intuition, the world becomes a place of connection, unity, and celebration.

Annabelle has supported hundreds of women to trust their inner guidance and rediscover their manifestation power.

If you're ready to harness your creative potential for a more peace-filled and abundant life, check out Annabelle's fourteen-day mini course at: www.annabellemerriman.com

Randall Monk

How has the Clickety-Clack shown up in your life?

The Clickety-Clack first showed up in my life in a major way when I was eighteen years old and about to graduate from high school. The Vietnam War and the draft were starting to come to the forefront of my mind. I was told at the time that if I got married, I would probably not be drafted. I do not know if this was true or not, but I did not feel like getting married at eighteen years old. I was also told that if I went to college, I probably would not be drafted. I was happy to have graduated from high school and not ready for college at that point.

I thought: *Geez, what am I going to do with this draft situation?* I did not want to go a strange country, fight in the war, and kill other human beings. Then I thought: *What would happen if I actually enlisted because I am going to be drafted anyway?* So that is what I ended up doing, enlisting.

Second, around 2003, my finances were not where I wanted them to be. I was in the mortgage business and making about $86,000 a year, and I knew I could do much better than that. The question was: *What can I do here?*

I had all the tools, but I had not really applied them in my life. I applied the ones I knew would work consistently and went from an annual income of $86,000 to $130,000 to $300,000 within a couple of years. I stayed consistent with my visualizations and my affirmations.

The next major challenge came when the company I was working for in the mortgage business went bankrupt. I was without a job and the mortgage business, even though it treated me well, was not my passion. I went through a process that I developed to discover my life purpose, and I found what my purpose is. Then, I went on to help people manage life's challenges, manifest their dreams, and discover their life purpose for themselves. I worked with people on the ascension process and ascension practices, and, from that content, I wrote my first book, *Life Mastery Tools for The Age of Ascension.*

Those were my three Clickety-Clack experiences.

How did you navigate the Clickety-Clack?

The challenge I had with the Vietnam War draft was to figure out what I was going to do. I decided to take the bull by horns and enlist in the Army because I wanted to serve. I asked the recruiter, "Can I choose what I want to do if I join the Army?"

And he said, "Yes, you can, as long as you pass the aptitude test."

I also asked him, "Can I choose where I will be stationed?"

He said, "Not exactly. You can request two places, but it is not a guarantee that you will be sent there."

Of course, I did not want to go to Vietnam, so I chose two other places. Japan was my first choice, and Germany was my second choice. I did end up going to Germany. What did I do? I followed the energy. That is what I did.

Second, I focused on creating $300,000 a year in income. Three times a day, I envisioned myself having that money. I held that energy throughout the day. That is how I managed to manifest that income.

Finally, when my corporate job crashed, I discovered my life purpose, and I moved on with my book. I wrote *Life Mastery Tools for The Age of Ascension*. I started leading workshops and webinars. Bottom line: I acted on my dreams. And with that, I was then able to live the life of my dreams.

What tools do you recommend for staying peaceful in a seemingly toxic world?

Well, there are several tools I recommend for staying peaceful in a seemingly toxic world. The first one is what I did when I joined the U.S. Army, knowing that I would be drafted if I did not do something. I followed the energy at that time, but I had no idea what I was doing. I understand it in retrospect. The energy was taking me in a direction, and I had to choose. I could let it flow and not take any control of it at all, or I could move with that energy rather than resist it.

There are always signs everywhere around us in our world. All we need to do is be consciously aware and follow that energy. In order to manifest, visualize, and hold that frequency, the feeling of the wish fulfilled. As Neville Goddard said, "Hold the feeling of the wish fulfilled."

When facing problems and the challenges in your world, look for the opportunities presented in the problem or challenge. There is always a gem within.

Finally, I would like to talk about transforming fear because there are a lot of people dealing with fear. This is a practice I have used successfully over the years, and it works quite well. First, acknowledge the fear. Do not ignore it; do not discount it. Do not try to push it or stuff it down. Acknowledge and experience the fear. Experience the feeling. That alone will normally dissipate the feeling to a degree, and sometimes totally.

From that experience, replace the feeling of fear with the feeling of love. Eventually you will be able to bring forth the feeling of love as soon as you notice fear rising up. That is a powerful exercise I have successfully used for years, and it can also be used for things like worry or other discordant energy. Acknowledge the feeling, experience it to a degree, and then replace it with love.

Last, I would like to recommend meditation. If you have the monkey mind and cannot meditate, then I suggest using guided meditation. Guided meditations are just as powerful, and that is a great way to manage life's challenges.

About the Author

Randall Monk is a student and teacher of self-help, ascension practices, metaphysics, and spiritual development. He has been studying subjects of this nature since the early 1970s and has been teaching them since 2007. Randall is the author of *Life Mastery Tools for The Age of Ascension*. He also co-authored the *Becoming an Alpha Master* audio program with Ronna Herman Vezane. For several years, he has been working closely with Ronna, a messenger for Archangel Michael.

Randall is a Prime Memory Seed Crystal Activator and, as such, works closely with a group of angels and special, encoded Seed Crystals. He also helps people discover their life purpose, manage life's challenges, and manifest their dreams via webinars and workshops.

For free guided meditations, visit his website: www. TimelyGuidance.com/shop.

Jason Michael Powers
and
Heather Grace Powers

How has the Clickety-Clack shown up in your life?

Jason: The Clickety-Clack has shown up in our lives in divorce. Both of us have experienced multiple divorces in our lives. In the times when love was dissolving around us, it brought up so much self-doubt, fear of love, fear of failure—that we felt like failures. However, these difficult times also brought up a knowing that there is this call in our life for love, for relationship—a knowing that we are built for relationship.

When those relationships around us were dissolving, it allowed us to be in a place of aloneness for a moment, wondering: *Will I ever reach that love that I know is in my heart, that which we call* divine love?

It afforded us the opportunity to shift from human love to divine love, and in that transitional time for each of us as we faced divorce, we found one another. A mentor of mine, Jim Lockard, said, "Two of the sacred cows that we have in our life in society is divorce is failure, and . . . marriage is forever."

We could watch life shift into another gear and awaken something else in both of us. The relationship is holy; it is a sacred container that holds this divine calling, this divine love. We had witnessed love dissolving around us in those difficult times, but that seed, that fire, that calling in our heart called us to find one another in that transitional time.

The transition was a very scary time, a lonely time. There is a time in the process of divorce that is like a chrysalis, a place of going within. It's the caterpillar stage of human love.

What is human love? Our views and practices have been programmed by our parents or TV or books.

When we find divine love, it is not from outside. It is something we find within. Those were scary times for both of us, the time of the Clickety-Clack, the time of transition when we were emerging from the caterpillar stage of human love to the butterfly stage of divine love.

How did you navigate the Clickety-Clack?

Heather: The journey navigating these darker places for us first involved a lot of deep self-work. When we came together, we had had enough experience with what felt like being mired in our mistakes, in failure, and in addiction. We both had a journey with addictive behavior. When we came together, we knew we wanted a partner who would have alliance with the other and be a champion to support growth in the grace of God.

We embodied a lot of shadow work going into our addictive behaviors, and it required a lot of self-love. What does that look like, to really love the holy, true self? Can we see how the small self, the limited self, is playing and causing things to continue in our shadows?

The most important place we came together was in prayer and in our devoted relationship with God. We recognized we were not able to have a full relationship without being centered in God, both individually and together. We made a commitment to demonstrate equality; we are both equal but not the same.

Being transparent and humble about our shortcomings with each other came with prayer. We knew that God would change us if we were honest with each other. Then we practiced acts of service in our life together. We discovered where our mess could become our message, where our struggles could become victories that could help other people down the same path of creating relationship within a spiritual practice.

What tools do you recommend for staying peaceful in a seemingly toxic world?

Jason: Well, for us, being in partnership is such an important piece, but our togetherness is an individual and united spiritual practice with one another. We talk about an evolutionary love, inspired by Andrew Harvey's work. That *evolutionary union* is one that allows us to border each other but not be invested in each other's circle. That individual and spiritual practice with one another is essential because sometimes we are solo islands. Having that shared spiritual practice, however, is what calls divine love into your life. It's what makes it possible to have that beloved relationship with the divine. *A cord of three strands is not easily broken*, as the Bible says (Ecclesiastes 4:12).

Spiritual practice is important, as well as being of service. Find service work you can do together; find a way you can serve as a couple. Service is outwardly focused. I think it was Saint-Exupéry who said, "Love does not consist in gazing at each other, but in looking outward together in the same direction" (Saint-Exupéry, Antoine, *Wind, Sand, and Stars*. 1939).

I mentioned evolutionary union. Committing to evolutionary union is a big part of entering relationship as a spiritual practice. Your relationship will evolve as an expression of that evolutionary impulse. You can sink into that really deep devotion to the Beloved presence of God, whatever that looks like for you, and join together in meditation and prayer.

Prayer is our first language. We have found whenever we get in trouble, our best step is to get on the prayer mat and come together in prayer—commune with the presence together. It seems like every time we do that, life tends to shift for the better.

Here is a simplified version of the indigenous Hawaiian prayer and ritual of Ho'oponopono (meaning *to set right*) I recommend to everybody:

Look into each other's eyes. Say within yourself:

> *I am sorry.*
>
> *Please forgive me.*
>
> *Thank you.*
>
> *I love you.*

About the Authors

Jason Michael and Heather Grace Powers are *The Powers of Love*. As musical artists, Evolutionary Relationship coaches, speakers, and authors, their music and message have been welcomed in countries all over the world and have touched thousands of lives.

Their passion is to support people through the awakening process and inspire, activate, and elevate more embodied Love on the planet, helping people create healthy, thriving, and balanced relationships. Through their own unfolding journey through the valleys and vistas, failures and victories of Love, they have discovered that relationships can be our greatest catalyst for change when we learn to shift our perception from being separate to seeing each other as allies on the journey with God at the center.

Their passion is fueled by believing that miracles happen, and relationships can become powerful portals of abundance, support, and healing for their families, their communities, and the world.

Learn more about Jason and Heather at www.ThePowersOfLove. com or visit their Facebook page: www.facebook.com/ thepowersoflove.

Lori Shen

How has the Clickety-Clack shown up in your life?

The Clickety-Clack showed up in my life when I was in my mid-twenties, while I was beginning to discover my mediumship abilities. I began developing these abilities in the mid 1990s, and for many years, there were no available teachers as no one was really talking about mediumship.

At times, I would see spirit people just walking around in everyday places like grocery stores, planes, or restaurants. Soon thereafter, they started showing up in my healing work. This pattern went on for many years, and I had to navigate all these experiences on my own until, finally, I found some classes that helped me understand what I was experiencing.

The first classes I took were not great, but then I discovered Arthur Findlay College, a world-renowned school for mediums, and the way I experienced my mediumship and spirit people completely changed. During an early class, a teacher told me that I was meant to be doing this professionally, but that meant I would not *see spirit people* in the way I had in the past. To be a more effective medium, I needed to *feel them*, and this would result in the spirit world stripping away my ability to see them the way I had previously. The spirit world was retraining me to work at a higher level, so that I could be trained properly from the ground up.

This process brought up all my fears and insecurities, like being wrong or embarrassed. I was thrown into the deep end in classes with great mediums who already seemed so advanced. I wanted to be in those classes, but I also wanted to hide in the background.

I never felt good enough because I was with people who had been training and already knew what they were doing. In my first class, I had to get up on stage in front of fifty people and deliver a reading. I had no idea what I was doing, but thankfully, somehow it worked.

How did you navigate the Clickety-Clack?

Once I started training with Arthur Findlay College, I had to have many talks with myself about going in with a beginner's mind and not comparing myself, my journey, or my level of ability to anyone else's. I constantly reminded myself to be inspired by these people who were more skilled than I and to learn from them. I am so thankful I did that because they really helped me.

I admired people in class who were bold and fearless and just went for it. They had some of the most powerful readings. One of those people who really inspired me said to me one day, "Lori, remember that saying: *Everything you want is on the other side of fear.*"

Those words have stuck with me because they are true. Whenever big fear comes up, I always know something extraordinary will come from it if I just walk through it. That is what I needed to do. I reminded myself of my intention for this work. That intention comes from a heart place and a healing place: *I want to be of service to both the spirit world and to the living, to help bring loved ones together.*

Mediumship is all about healing and the opportunity for people to be with their loved ones in spirit, one more time. I had to focus on my intention. My work is not about me; it is about being the best I can be to bring these two worlds together, this love connection back together. That focus helped me get out of my own way. Instead of beating myself up, I gave myself permission to make mistakes in my classes. I changed my perspective and started looking at those mistakes as opportunities. Whenever I would receive a no or something went wrong, it was an opportunity for some great lessons that ultimately taught me to be a better medium.

Finally, I worked at mastering my craft. Practice, practice, practice—as much as I could. I also learned to trust that the Universe and Spirit always have my back and want me to do well. They want this energy exchange to happen, and they always support me. So, it is a matter of trusting in Spirit.

What tools do you recommend for staying peaceful in a seemingly toxic world?

For staying peaceful, I am a big believer in practicing **gratitude** and counting your blessings, every single day. There are always things to be grateful for. We all have blessings, no matter what our circumstances are. I start my day with gratitude. I end my day with gratitude, and I try to practice it throughout the day, as it keeps me in a peaceful place and makes life flow. If you are grateful, you will feel more in the flow with your spirit, more in alignment.

I also recommend **meditation**. Meditation helps move your body, mind, and spirit into alignment.

Some of the benefits of meditation are:

- It grants you access to your personal guidance system.
- It helps you gain clarity.
- It helps you stay centered.
- It grounds you.
- It connects you with your higher self and your Spirit team.

You can use meditation to guide you into asking questions that lead to life answers.

Make **time and space** for yourself. People do not do that enough. We need to feel centered and balanced in our lives.

Be **intentional** with your heart and soul, reminding yourself of your intentions: why you are doing things, why you are with the people you are with.

Finally, surround yourself with **great people** who love, respect, and support you and your dreams and goals, people who share a reciprocal connection with you.

About the Author

Lori Shen is an internationally known Psychic Medium, Energy Healer, and Space Clearing Practitioner with certifications in clinical hypnotherapy, past-life regression, Reiki, and psychic mediumship. Over the past twenty-five years, she has devoted herself to studies in spirituality, metaphysics, and a wide variety of body, mind, and spirit healing modalities. She has studied with experts affiliated with institutions around the world, including the renowned Arthur Findlay College.

Based in the San Francisco Bay Area, Lori mentors individuals and leads group readings in the fields of energy healing and psychic and mediumistic development. She integrates intuitive abilities with practical techniques from her background to help people make powerful shifts, enabling them to pursue more joyful and healthy lives. Her passion and ability to enrich and empower the lives of others is recognized by peers and clients alike.

To connect with Lori, you can message her through her website: www.lorishen.com.

Genevieve Siegel

How has the Clickety-Clack shown up in your life?

A couple of years ago, my year started well, career-wise. I was part of a Wellness Leadership Academy (WLA) master's program and was on my way to becoming an advanced teacher for the Arvigo® Therapy. I was traveling around the world, making a lot of money, and seeing a lot of clients. I went to a couple of immersion events with WLA, and I felt like something was a little off.

I am an extroverted empath, so I knew I was feeling somebody's stuff. Needless to say, I had a pit in my stomach. I would think *okay* and kind of toss it off. I believed somebody was releasing something, not a big deal. I moved on. Then later in that year, in the exact same week, I went to an advanced teacher meeting for the Arvigo® Therapy. We were there to meet with all the teachers and the owners to have a good time and go over professional stuff we needed to do.

The owner decided to drop the bomb that she needed to step back and was going to sell the company. Everybody in the room—there were probably eighteen of us—was devastated and felt lost. We were afraid, anxious, and crying, and I was engulfed by everything. The same week, I received a call from my mentor from WLA who told me she was leaving WLA to pursue her career and some personal things in her life.

I felt: *Oh my God! Here we go, another thing.* I felt like my world was completely imploding. I did not know what I was going to do. I wanted to finish the master's program, but I had been with this mentor for a good eight months, meeting with her every other week.

I felt the Clickety-Clack, and I felt everybody else's Clickety-Clack. I did not know what I was going to do. I felt my path was no longer there. I went home and allowed myself to completely process everything that was happening. I allowed myself to feel because I am very empathic. I cried. I stomped my feet. I made space so I could scream. I tried to tap into what was really going on, asking: Is this all mine? Am I feeling all of this? Am I lost with all that is happening?

How did you navigate the Clickety-Clack?

I went home after hearing devastating news about both of my worlds: the company being sold and my mentor leaving. I felt as if there was something still going on in the WLA as a company, so I went home and made sure I felt everything. I expressed everything, processed every emotion out. I felt the fear, I felt the anxiety, I felt the anger, and then allowed myself to let them go.

I asked myself: *Is this really going to serve me?* I realized a lot of the emotions were not necessarily mine, but those of the other teachers and mentors at the WLA. I was feeling all their stuff as well because the teachers at the Arvigo® Institute had put all their eggs in one basket. The institute was their livelihood.

I realized I had other things going on like WLA. I had been teaching and I had my practice that was going well. So, I used my holistic self-care techniques. I did reflexology and trades and got regular massages. I did my neuro-linguistic programming (NLP) with my teacher, clearing all those negative beliefs and fears I had about money and believing in myself. I hunkered down and danced and did all the things that were holistically healthy for me.

I continued with my master's program. I learned from other WLA mentors, who were fabulous. I did as much as I possibly could. I continued teaching and supporting my clients. As a result, I ended up creating a new website. I created the Gen-Touch Holistic Fertility Method™ program for my fertility clients. I continued empowering all my clients to be calm, confident, and in control of their fertility or their holistic health journeys.

I helped my fertility clients through the digital hybrid program I developed. Then I took that program, filmed and edited everything myself, created an online program, and put it on my website. It ended up being one of the highest income years of my holistic health career. A year later, many of we teachers who were previously devastated got together and created Abdominal Therapy Collective Incorporated, an international holistic education corporation.

I realized what was mine and what was not. I kept doing what I needed to do and came out the other side quite successfully.

What tools do you recommend for staying peaceful in a seemingly toxic world?

I have developed a lot of different tools for myself that I share with my clients. One of them I call the Triple L Method™: List, Let Go, and Listen. I am very visual, and I am often in my head. I list everything I am feeling, thinking, and sensing. I list everything else that is going on mentally, emotionally, physically, and spiritually.

Then, I give myself permission to let it go, and I either throw it away, toss it away like a basketball, or burn it. I love safely burning things. I get rid of it somehow. I keep doing that process until those thoughts and emotions are clear and away from my head. There is something about writing it down that takes the feeling away, and I think: *It is in a safe space. I do not have to think about that anymore.*

Next, I listen to the signs of my body. Listen to my spirit. Listen to my intuition. Listen to my inner knowing. We each have our higher selves, and we have all the answers that we need. If not, we can connect to Divine Source, our guides, and our angels. How I do that is to create a nice safe space, drop a nice energetic bubble around myself, and know that everything I release will be going to a safe space.

Finally, I give myself permission to receive things. You may write down the question you want to ask to the Divine beforehand so you do not have to stress that you will not remember it. Ask the question, then quiet your mind. I usually do guided meditations.

I have some for my clients on YouTube, so they can enter that safe space and clear out everything. I realize that women and men meditate differently. You can find your own way to meditate and clear and quiet your mind. Then, you can connect with the Divine.

You may connect to nature or use divination cards like animal spirit or tarot cards. You can pray. I also like to dance and be open to connect with my guides, my angels, or Source. Remember to give yourself permission to receive the answers.

If you do not receive anything, that is okay too. Maybe you just need to quiet your mind, to relax. The next time you might be more open and receive an answer. Then trust. Trust those answers. Trust in the Divine or Source, and trust in yourself.

About the Author

Genevieve Siegel was a corporate accountant for thirteen years and ended that career because of debilitating panic attacks. She went to Holistic Healing School, healed, transformed her life, awakened her soul, and found her new calling. For sixteen years, she has empowered people who were having reproductive issues and helped them to feel calm, confident, and in control of their reproductive health journey.

She has a special passion for empowering people globally, so they can be their whole, healthy, and happy selves again. Genevieve is a Holistic Health Empowerment Diva and an Educator for the Abdominal Therapy Collective. She is the owner of Gen-Touch Holistics. With her holistic approach and a passion for facilitating the growth and healing of others, soon Genevieve will be empowering people to Own Your Merde™ through her new Holistic Health Program to honor all your sides—the good, the bad, the ugly, and the beautiful.

If you would like to receive a free relaxation and meditation MP3 or learn more about the new Own Your Merde™ Program, visit www.gentouchholistics.com or contact her at gen@gentouchholistics.com.

Sarah Spann

How has the Clickety-Clack shown up in your life?

The Clickety-Clack has shown up in a lot of ways, but there are two I want to share. The first time I was quite young, in my teenage years. I was experiencing a lot of gut pain all the time. I was unwell, very underweight, was even hospitalized. My health was in a downward spiral, and no one could figure out what was wrong. After several years, I was diagnosed with celiac disease.

That diagnosis kick-started my healing journey for my physical health. Through that experience, I started to learn more about nutrition and what was right for my body. There was a big learning curve, and it was quite a difficult time physically.

The second time was more recently, when I started my business in nutritional medicine, helping people with gut problems, going forward from my own experience. I was pushing myself really, really hard to get it going and to make it successful. I ended up at a point where I could not push myself anymore; I could not continue to pump things out the way I was. That was the wakeup call for me to heal at another level, an emotional one. Of course, it was impacting my physical health.

These were the two times I was stopped in my tracks and needed to reassess how I was doing things in order to deepen my healing.

How did you navigate the Clickety-Clack?

When I was physically unwell, I tried to figure out what was going on. I tried different things with my diet, I prioritized my health, and I started to exercise and take care of myself a bit better. Once I received the diagnosis, I learned what it means to have celiac disease and was able to cut out gluten. I prioritized my health and focused on getting myself well. That focus helped me navigate because I had something to work towards, and I began to see results that motivated me to keep going.

At one point, I realized I was pushing myself too hard in my business, and my health was suffering again. I wanted to keep pushing forward, but my body would not let me. I needed to surrender to the process and once again look after my health. I reassessed how I was doing things and bumped up my self-care. I focused internally and reconnected with myself on a spiritual and emotional level, asking myself what I really needed in this time.

I slowly let myself take care of myself a little better and let happen what needed to happen. I let go of how I was doing things. At the end of the day, I surrendered and tried to give my body what it needed. I also softened up and started asking people for help and support, and then I allowed people to support me.

What tools do you recommend for staying peaceful in a seemingly toxic world?

First, ensure your inside matches your outside. If you are someone like me, who is good at projecting peace and calm while there is chaos inside, it will catch up to you in other ways. For me, it caught me in my health. Process what you are feeling—by journaling, talking to someone, or exercising. If you are particularly angry, you might need to punch the air or do a strong workout. Make sure you have internal harmony and are not holding your feelings inside, pretending everything is fine.

The next thing that really helped me is grounding. I do it every single day. I walk barefoot on the grass in my backyard, which I am fortunate to have. Any patch of grass is fine; just ground yourself, breathe deeply, and bring yourself into the present moment as often as you can. Even if you take a quick walk around for five minutes, you will be amazed at how much it can calm you, especially when things are difficult.

Another tool I find powerful is practicing gratitude, particularly when I am feeling overwhelmed. In a difficult moment, I think of three things I am grateful for. It dissipates the overwhelm so I can gain a bit of perspective. Overwhelm often causes us to feel unbalanced and moves us into our heads a bit, so everything feels like it is piling up.

Bringing yourself back into a gratitude state helps dissipate overwhelm and gives you a better perspective to move forward. Again, it's important to open up and allow yourself to be supported. Do not pretend all is fine, and remember to look out for your own self-care.

About the Author

Sarah Spann is a holistic wellness practitioner and writer based in Queensland, Australia. She is best known for her innovative work in gut health and her first book, *Mind the Gut*. As an author, speaker, clinical nutritionist, Reiki practitioner, and wellness coach, Sarah works closely with her clients to uncover the root cause of their illness and heal holistically. Sarah's passion is empowering people to nurture themselves back to their most vibrant health so they can thrive.

Sarah's qualifications include a Bachelor of Health Science (Nutritional Medicine), Advanced Diploma of Nutritional Medicine, Shamanic Reiki Level 1, and wellness coach training.

Sarah has also been featured in many online outlets, including *Healthline*, *Health Magazine UK*, Humanley, Light Warrior Radio, eHealth Radio Network, and Ticker TV. She also served as an editor for *Surviving Prostate Cancer*.

To learn more about Sarah and her work, or to get in touch, head to her website sarahspann.net or find her on Instagram @ therealsarahspann.

Steph St. Amand

How has the Clickety-Clack shown up in your life?

The Clickety-Clack has shown up in my life as a lack of confidence in who I am and in what the energy of the Divine has created in me. So, the Clickety-Clack showed up as fear: fear of rejection, fear of failure, and fear of spiritual trolls. The beautiful adventure of my life has been to find peace, to find worthiness and value in who I am. My life has been a big adventure of being, of waking up and saying thank you—an expression of Spirit in life.

The Clickety-Clack showed up through food addiction and the journey of recovery from that addiction. The Clickety-Clack in my life has been fear of not saying the right things or being in the right person or being the right light at the right time in the mosaic of life. It has been an interesting adventure, working through that awareness of even noticing where the Clickety-Clack shows up as the stuff that blocks or hinders the growth and the evolution of the Divine soul that is the living breathing entity and identity within each of us, within that radiant I AM that is the expression of Spirit unfolding.

Fear builds up and makes us afraid of unleashing our light, the expression of our true divine selves. People often talk about a *monkey mind* or a *hamster brain*. I have always said that there is monkey playing with the hamster inside my brain!

I took the opportunity to quiet and still that expression of the Clickety-Clack. It was rampant in my mind. I wanted a gentle awakening and always ended up with a loud, booming voice.

How did you navigate the Clickety-Clack?

There was a distinct moment in my life. I have moments of sitting upright in my bed and hearing that booming voice of a divine voice, of God, of Spirit, or maybe my Higher Self. I woke up one day and realized that fear was invading my life, holding me hostage and taking advantage of me. I turned to fear and imagined it as a relationship that was not working.

It was an abusive relationship. I simply turned to fear, and I broke up with it. I kicked fear to the curb. My favorite acronym came to me in that moment: Face Everything And Roar (FEAR). That moment led me to a beautiful opening. I did not let fear dictate who I was to become or who I was to be in the world. Instead, I chose a beautiful expression of the growth and expansion of being to navigate my life. I chose to show up as the light I am and to spark the expression of the message and meaning of this life that is uniquely qualified to expand through me.

Everyone must recognize their own wholeness, their oneness with this Divine infinite mind and expansion and evolution of the soul. They must choose to be their light, their unique and unrepeatable expression. That means breaking up with fear and kicking it to the curb. We must allow trust within us of our wholeness, trusting the Universe to expand and grow us.

I am enough. I am enough, and that is what I see in everyone. Every single person on this planet is enough.

What tools do you recommend for staying peaceful in a seemingly toxic world?

The first step in everything is to do nothing. Do not react or respond. Take a moment and take a breath in stillness to be present with the now that is happening.

I love to do this practice because of the monkey-hamster mind that is in me. I call it *affirmation bombardment*. When I catch myself being negative or thinking the opposite of my truth, I bombard my mind with affirmations. If my mind cannot deliver them, I make sure there are other voices in my life that are affirmative, positive, and uplifting. So, there is only affirmative bombardment in my mind. That is one of my favorite tools.

Another tool is to be consistent in spiritual practice. It is not called spiritual *doneness*; it is called spiritual *practice*. So we practice every day until we wake up, until the fullness of Spirit is expanding who we are as *enoughness*, as wholeness, and as love. That spiritual practice is necessary and so vital to a life of fulfillment and of peace.

During a fear moment, I woke up and said thank you for the first time. That was the birth of *Wake Up, Say Thank You*. I have done consistent spiritual practice—on Facebook Live—for over four years. Oh my goodness! I am the blessed one; I am the lucky one people click on a button to see. That is ridiculously humbling.

God told me to teach this, God told me to love them, and God told me to serve love. When you are called by a higher purpose, fear is the one thing you need to remove from your energy field because your message needs to be out there. There is too much fear in the world, and we need to be fearlessly interacting with our true selves.

About the Author

Steph St. Amand is an ordained minister with Centers for Spiritual Living, is an international speaker, and is the cofounding Spiritual Director of 1 Love Awakening, a global virtual community bridging hearts, awakening minds, and transforming lives. With a mission to cultivate radical joy and empower unconditional self-acceptance, Rev. Steph exploded onto the social media scene in 2017 with *Wake Up! Say Thank You!* a Facebook live weekday Spiritual Practice to provide spiritual nourishment for the heart, mind, and soul, now in its fifth year.

You can find more of Steph St. Amand at www.1LoveAwakening.com, or join in spiritual practice, weekdays on Facebook or YouTube at @1LoveAwakening.

Laurie St Clare

How has the Clickety-Clack shown up in your life?

May I present 2020? I know the pandemic has been tough for a lot of people and has been the backdrop for everybody. For me, it started out New Year's Day when my father died. Death is always difficult, so it was a bittersweet thing. It was definitely an indicator of how my year was going to roll out.

In February, I got COVID. I was extremely sick, and I had a near-death experience. The next month, I was notified that I had been selected to be in a project I wanted to be in. Just a few weeks later, I was notified that the project was shelved because of the pandemic. The possibility of it coming back was also dependent on what happened with COVID.

The next month, I was thinking I very much wanted to move, but I did not want to during all the craziness. However, my friend was nearly killed in a car crash a few weeks later. I then decided to pack up my stuff and get out of Los Angeles. I went to northern California to help her get to all her doctor's appointments. While I was there, my brother died.

I was pretty much a wreck because I was used to helping everybody else, and I now needed help. I was out of my comfort zone and stability. It was a lot to happen all in such a short span of time. The year 2020 was a good representation of the

Clickety-Clack, especially in Los Angeles during the pandemic with everything going on.

How did you navigate the Clickety-Clack?

I let myself be vulnerable. I reached out to friends, and I let people help me. I am usually a person who would say to herself: *I am strong. I can handle this. I can do this.* I am always reaching out to help others, and this was a time where I had to accept help and be open to other people's support.

I am an astrologer; I am also a medium. I looked at my own astrological chart, and I had to take my own advice. If my advice is good enough to give to other people, it had to be good enough to give myself. I took time for myself. I looked at what was going on for me, astrologically, and I also had readings from other mediums.

I can connect with my loved ones who have passed, but when in grief it is much harder to do that. I allowed other people to do that for me, bringing me peace and helping me through that time. Giving myself permission to take the time I needed to heal and letting myself be in a down period was important. I let myself have rest. I let myself be nurtured by others.

What tools do you recommend for staying peaceful in a seemingly toxic world?

I always recommend being grounded. This is one of the things I do daily. Most people recommend going out into nature, which is fantastic. There's nothing better than that as it helps you get back to Source. But there are times you cannot go into nature. You can use your mind to ground and visualize, see yourself sitting on a tree trunk, for example.

Having that grounding, that connection to the earth, is so important. To ground, you can use your mind to visualize yourself sitting on a tree trunk. Consider grounding as similar to electricity; you need a ground so you do not get shocked, so you do not blow a fuse. That is a great analogy, right? There are so many opportunities for us to blow fuses.

Another tool I use is astrology, and I have been using it since a young age. Astrology helps me see the bigger picture and understand why something is happening—to see its purpose. It always makes me think of the Bible passage in Ecclesiastes 3:1: "To everything there is a season, and a time for every purpose under heaven." The Byrds made a song out of it, "Turn! Turn! Turn!" I am not particularly religious, but the Bible has great passages whether you are religious or not.

I always look to the heavens. I look to the stars to find the purpose of what is happening in order to move through situations with grace, balancing intellect and intuition.

About the Author

Laurie St Clare is an internationally known astrologer, medium, and healer. Interested in metaphysics at a young age, Laurie has pursued her passion for many decades. Following the tragic death of her brother when she was ten, she set herself on a path to understand the connection between people and the connection between this life and the next.

Laurie is a Master of Evolutionary Astrology, practicing the astrology of freedom and freewill to help her clients live their most empowered life. She is also a natural born medium as well as being extensively trained by the top mediums in their field. She has studied at the world-famous Arthur Findlay College in the United Kingdom.

She has been featured on the well-known radio show hosted by Michael and Raphaelle Tamura, *Living the Miracle*. Laurie enjoys working with clients one-on-one and speaking at spiritual circles and women's retreats.

To reach Laurie St Clare go to: www.lauriestclare.com or @Laurie St Clare on Instagram.

Trey Stinnett

How has the Clickety-Clack shown up in your life?

The Clickety-Clack has shown up in my life in a lot of ways, typically when I was going through a transition in my career. Most notably, the Clickety-Clack showed up in my life after the passing of my father.

I got an early start in business. Working with my father in real estate, I'd reached millionaire status at only twenty-one. But in the crash of 2008, we lost everything. And just two years later—the year I was married—my dad passed away. This kick-started multiple years of depression. I gained forty-five pounds and couldn't hold down a job, let alone make a business work. It got so bad, I had to sell my grandfather's coin collection and my wife's car just to make rent.

I can remember being at rock bottom, trying to figure out some way to earn money online at one o' clock in the morning. I washed Ritalin down with Red Bull, trying to figure things out. I was grinding, and I was not able to be the present father I wanted to be. I needed to make that shift, that transition out of the Clickety-Clack.

Being at rock bottom can sometimes give you massive amounts of perspective. That period of my life, ending around age twenty-eight to twenty-nine, is when I began to find the tools and the ability to navigate my way out of the Clickety-Clack.

How did you navigate the Clickety-Clack?

The interesting thing about rock bottom is there is nowhere to go but up. It had been four years since my dad had passed and six since the market had crashed. I looked to the only thing I could think of to help me navigate my way out of the rut I was in— books. Books had helped me pull myself out of college to start my first business, to make my first million, and I hoped maybe they could help me pull myself out of depression too.

During my depression, I had come to the conclusion that none of my previous successes were real—I had a lot of negative self-talk. When one of the authors I had been reading, Tim Ferriss, started his podcast, I became an avid listener. Guest after guest would come on to his show and share their story. It seemed to me they all had one thing in common: meditation. I had no idea what I was doing, but for the first time in my life, I sat down in my backyard, closed my eyes, and started counting my breaths. Within weeks, it was like a portal opened to a completely new reality for me.

I went on a tear of discovering and seeking the tools that would lead me to self-awareness. At the time, I did not know what to call it. I thought it was self-improvement. I went to Tony Robbins, then to Landmark, and then to Burning Man. I went to the Sacred Valley of the Incas in Peru and did hallucinogenic plant medicines with shamans to try to find answers that would help me understand how to be the best person I could be and how to release trauma.

By the end of that year, I shed the forty-five pounds I had gained, my income recovered to higher levels than ever before, I rekindled my relationships with my wife and my mother, and my life was finally on an upward trajectory again. The journey has not been without challenges and certainly not without mistakes. But that was my shift out of the Clickity-Clack.

I continually discover more and more tools for what I call *radical self-awareness*, the intention to always understand who we are at a subtle level, at a body level. It's the gift that keeps on giving: The more self-awareness we bring into our lives, the more we find we are removing things rather than adding them in. There is a lot of junk going on inside our bodies, our hearts, and our minds. Becoming more and more radically self-aware is like building a muscle. We are no longer driven by our traumas, and we become truly free to choose.

What tools do you recommend for staying peaceful in a seemingly toxic world?

Staying peaceful in a seemingly toxic world requires stepping outside of that toxic world, and the master tool I recommend for this is **radical self-awareness**.

Next, before any tool can be applied, we need to understand there is a space in between what happens to us and how we respond to it. Typically, we do not recognize that space, and we react immediately to what is happening in the news, in the media, in our job, and in our relationships. Often, that reaction is not coming from choice. It is coming from an accumulation of micro-traumas throughout our life, an accumulation of beliefs we have picked up from the reality that we have lived in.

When you can understand there is a link between your feelings and your thoughts, your thoughts and your actions, then you can discover how to have more choice in your life. The more choice you have, the more your health shifts, the more your relationships shift, and the more your wealth shifts. As a teacher of wealth, I have made it my mission to help people discover personal transformation through that channel.

It does not matter if we are going in to work specifically on wealth; the other areas of life end up being addressed as well. Because what creates a lot of the challenges, conflicts, and friction—causing us to be out of flow—is often not what we are *doing*, but the beliefs and thoughts driving our actions.

I've discovered so many tools over the years that I now have an entire course to take people through. In it, I share all the tools, train my students how to use them, and help them adopt these tools into their lives.

They look at the three areas:

1. *The outer world*—We examine their actions to determine which are in *flow* and which are a *grind*. We all have different personalities, so really understanding what makes us different is key.

2. *The inner world*—We explore how to live a purpose-filled life that is also sustainable. Most of the time, we are either doing things we care about or doing things that make us money. The key is integrating both—what we care about that also makes us money—aligning our work with our passion.

3. *The spiritual world*—We tune in to living in a vibration of abundance.

I use these tools every single day in my own life. I practice abundance vibration hygiene. I make sure the actions I am taking are in flow with my personality type. I have completely designed my life to keep me aligned with my purpose.

I created a free quiz that allows you to measure whether you are in flow, so you can take immediate actions on all three of these levels: the outer world, the inner world, and the spiritual world. Find the quiz at: flowquiz.biz.

About the Author

Trey Stinnett, a.k.a. "The Flow Coach," is the host of *The Hustle & Heal* podcast, in which highly successful entrepreneurs share the insights and tools they use to achieve mastery of wealth through mastery of self.

Co-founder of The Alliance of Conscious Entrepreneurs (ACE), Trey and his wife, Grace, empower business owners to build a bioidentical business so they can achieve their full wealth potential while living a life they love.

Trey is excited to show others the tools of radical self-awareness he's assembled for the entrepreneurs in his community. He works with clients interested in carving their own life-path outside the seemingly toxic world, clients who believe that owning their own business is the best way to do that.

To start with a free Flow Quiz to help identify if you are out of flow and what immediate steps you can take to get back into flow where you work less, make more money, and maximize your impact on the world, go to: flowquiz.biz.

Nicole Thibodeau

How has the Clickety-Clack shown up in your life?

The Clickety-Clack is often present during simultaneous life transitions. Some transitions are tougher ones, and some are easier to get through. The attitude we choose toward these moments makes the whole difference. Sometimes we do not have any choice in making them happen, but the attitude we take toward them changes everything, changes the outcome.

I was about to go on maternity leave. I was eight months pregnant, and I was going for a two-year maternity sabbatical, without pay. Then, my husband lost his job. The company was closing down, and the employees received a little bit of money, but not much. We could not touch that money because it was being invested. I was quite uncomfortable, as I wanted to stay home with my baby for two years.

I started speaking affirmations and looking out the window. My words became a mantra: *God provides for all birds, and so will He for us.* We began discussing what would be next because it was a difficult time. We had just bought a house, and we did not want to move back into an apartment. Those were really tough moments to deal with, especially being fully pregnant with my hormones all the way to the top.

How did you navigate the Clickety-Clack?

My husband always dreamed of starting his own company, so we started discussing how that could be possible. Starting a business while giving birth at the same time is not easy. We agreed that I would assist him because I had an accounting background, and the paperwork would be easier for me.

Then, we reached out to experts who help young entrepreneurs start up a business and create a business plan. Meanwhile, I had our baby. As we were filling out those papers, I would nurse the baby and then hand over the baby to my husband. While he was holding the baby, I would continue typing in everything. It was a team effort—together with experts—and we managed to prepare our business plan and apply for a grant to start our business.

Even though it was not a lot of money, it was enough for us to start and secure new clients coming into the new business. Of course, having faith—always asking God for guidance—is the way I always did things. We managed to navigate that Clickety-Clack. I was able to stay on my maternity leave for two years.

The communication between my husband and me was also important because it kept us going and trusting in each other, so we could accomplish our dreams.

What tools do you recommend for staying peaceful in a seemingly toxic world?

Breathing consciously helps me a lot, and it also helps a lot of other people.

There is **meditation**. I do active meditation, not sitting down. My mind is too busy; I need to be doing something else.

I use **toning**. I use the *Om* sound; I sing it in different tonalities to feel the vibration in my body. Toning helps to bring my body back into alignment.

I also use **affirmations**, and the books I used were the Joseph Murphy spiritual books and Ronna Herman Vezane, who channels the Archangel Michael. These books carried me throughout these difficult moments because they uplifted my energy.

Give yourself **permission to change**, as that allows the change to happen with ease and grace. It helps to trust the process of change as well.

Connect these practices to your sacred heart. We all have Divine energy, our Divine self, living within our heart. It is important to come back to your center, to your Divine heart, and connect deeply to it. That is where you sit, and it is your safe haven, where you can reconnect with the Divine and let go of what is happening outside of you. Then, you can just focus on what needs to be done in the moment instead of having your mind scattered in different directions. The connection helps realign your body and mind so they can bring the changes for the highest good in your life at that moment.

About the Author

Nicole Thibodeau is an Oracle of Divine Transmissions. As a Channeler and Mentor, she works with spiritually evolving, gentle souls blossoming into their healing gifts and on their spiritual path, so they can have more clarity and be in liberty to live their divinity. She is most passionate about assisting gentle souls to embrace their Divine power and become the masters of their lives.

She offers her own programs, Unveil Your Inner Gifts™ and Embrace Your Divine Power™, as well as soul-healing sessions and channelings for groups.

She uses Light language, toning, and creates codes—images infused with high frequencies—to assist her clients to activate energies in a remarkably simple, gentle, and yet powerful way.

You can connect with Nicole at:

Her website: www.nicolethibodeau.ca

Facebook: facebook.com/nicolethibodeau.ca

Instagram: nicolethibodeau.ca

Email: info@nicolethibodeau.ca

You can find the Peaceful Heart Principles she uses regularly to recenter and keep herself in a state of Divine peace at: tinyurl. com/NCC3PeacefulHeart.

Marie-Laure Will

How has the Clickety-Clack shown up in your life?

I was working at the top level of a large company, a tech company. I had been dismissed, fired from the company. I was not fired for incompetencies but for economic reasons. The dismissal was very sudden, and it was a big shock. I lost everything. I lost my social stature. I lost my social badge. I lost my car, my company car. I lost all my duties and my computer.

This was a difficult period of my life because that was my first failure. Everything I had been doing was a big success. I had quantum success, and that was amazing to a lot of people, but I didn't realize that. Suddenly I didn't not know what to do with my life, or what to say to my family, because this was a big shame for me. My ego was hurt, and I was completely lost in my life. It was a big transition.

How did you navigate the Clickety-Clack?

I decided not to go to another company. In fact, I made a choice to be trained as an executive coach. I set up my own company of sustainable technology for entrepreneurs and CEOs, to help them increase their value proposition face with investors. It was big success at the beginning and also a big challenge. It was like a renewal in my life. At the same time, it was not new for me, because my parents—all my family in fact—and my grandparents were founders of their own and successful industries.

In my professional career, I had experienced the industry of high technology semiconductors at a top level. I created a way to complete the two industries and to propose to entrepreneurs in the field they work to grow their companies in high tech and sustainable development. I excelled in this area. I had two associates. It was a great, great experience.

I did not sit down and cry. I knew my own character and deep personality, so I said: *Okay, I am a failure there, but what can I do today to renew and reinvent myself into something else closer to me?* I sat down to meditate and check with my angel. I asked: *What can I do with God? What can I do to contribute to the world? What would I love to do?*

I decided to set up my own company.

What tools do you recommend for staying peaceful in a seemingly toxic world?

Have faith in life and faith in yourself. Have a clear goal and clear vision. I don't think we are here by chance on Earth. We are on Earth for a mission, an important soul mission, and we need our life to be aligned with this whole mission. Otherwise, we might derail from our true purpose of life on Earth, which changes the trajectory of our soul. The trajectory of our soul brings inner security in the world, in the society where we live. It affects how we move and think when we know the goal of our soul.

I have created by my own method and process to find the soul's trajectory and align it with body, heart, and the spirit-mind. This process involves more than sitting and meditating for a while. It is great to meditate from my perspective. However, it is important to contribute to the world and to serve other people and our own soul. Our soul's mission is both at the same time. To make a difference in the world requires real effort.

The more we align our soul trajectory, the more work we accomplish in our real life because the Universe responds to our Divine life on Earth if we make this effort. After this life, there is a renewal of life. Our frequency of vibration increases more and more as we move to higher levels.

In your true nature, you do not need to think in a complex way. It is easy to focus on an idea and ask if it is aligned with your higher self. If it is in alignment, it will be perfectly embodied in what you manifest in your reality, the world. You don't need to develop complex thinking or conduct a lot of research; you simply take life as it is and let the flow circulate. The right person is coming, the right situation is arising, and we will be spectators who see the right results, all aligned with our soul mission.

About the Author

Thanks to a powerful energetic gift revealed in Israel on the Mount of Olives, Marie-Laure guides high-caliber leaders and celebrities to make great breakthroughs in a ten-fold shorter time.

If you want to quickly align your life with the trajectory of your soul and live a life of full passion and abundance without putting in tons of effort, contact Marie-Laure Will on her website and accept her special offer for "Le Saut Quantique d'Abondance" (The Quantum Leap of Abundance) at: www.marielaurewill. com.

Gretchen Wilson

How has the Clickety-Clack shown up in your life?

The Clickety-Clack has shown up in my life twice in the last eight years. It is as if the last eight years have been a bit of a barbell with the Clickety-Clack starting back in 2013 and 2014 and then coming into the present with the pandemic in 2020 and 2021. Back in 2013, I made a decision to leave corporate financial services after twenty-three years. I felt I had learned all I could. I had been given great opportunities across phenomenal companies, and I had worked across several functional areas and learned how businesses were built. I felt I needed more in order to grow.

In 2013, I decided to leave without knowing where I was going. I moved into the startup world at that point, a little bit of a pivot from financial services. The startup I was involved with was a custom craft brewery with a novel concept in the brewery space.

I reconnected with someone I knew briefly when I was working at John Hancock, and he and his wife had come up with an incredible concept. I felt as though their business model was happening at the right time, and it was fortuitous that I happened to watch their LinkedIn video. I hardly ever watched videos those days, but I decided to pay attention to a video that this guy had sent out.

After seven months of helping the brewery get up and running, I returned to corporate financial services in the form of consulting. As I was consulting, I started to feel I was out of my element, out of control. I felt overwhelmed by what I was tackling. I felt at a loss with the transition, and a lot of noise and a negative voice were happening in my head. This Clickety-Clack started to impact me.

In 2018, my sister found out that she had cancer, and over the course of the next year we discovered it was metastatic cancer. In 2020, COVID hit, and that year was extremely challenging across the board: my brother experienced heart problems and my brewery failed. Early in 2021, my brother passed away and a startup that I had subsequently began dissolved.

These are the two areas where the Clickety-Clack has shown up in my life.

How did you navigate the Clickety-Clack?

I knew the negative voice in my head was my biggest challenge, so I started to immerse myself in education. I read everything I could. My reading took me down paths of mental brain function, negative voices, overcoming negative voices, retraining habits, neuroscience, psychology, and spirituality.

Despite the fact that this information came from different angles, something was coming together. It had to do with developing the power within myself to grow and become. I continued to explore opportunities; I educated myself in a host of different areas. I reconnected with financial services. I was advising start-ups and started leading projects for industry groups, speaking to industry groups and universities. I followed all my networking leads.

I changed my habits. I became aware of what I was doing and what was triggering my behavior. In the Clickety-Clack, I had been drinking more, so I reduced the drinking. I went back to running and spent much more time alone.

Finally, I realized what I wanted to share with the world. I co-authored and self-published a book for startup founders, *Launch! 11 Key Elements of Wildly Successful Startups*, to help others learn without taking as much time as I did to learn many of the lessons in the startup world.

What tools do you recommend for staying peaceful in a seemingly toxic world?

First of all, I am a huge fan of **meditation**. Taking the opportunity to quiet the mind needs to be done, and I refer to this as *recentering my personal GPS*. What I have come to realize is that we need to do this every day. Throughout the day, our environments influence us, people influence us, and we do not realize how much we can stray and be taken off course. I use each morning as an opportunity to reset my GPS. I start with meditation, and then I read because I do not wake up every morning springing out of bed, ready to take on the world. I need to reenergize, and I need to find power within to bring forth what I am meant to do each day.

Second, I live by a motto: **Live to give**. People are always giving. Some people give things to us, and we need to be gracious and accept. However, there are some things that might not be what we are after, and we should accept the gift of knowing whether it is the correct direction. Everyone is here to provide a learning opportunity and to help guide us along the way. By giving each day, I point someone in a direction, and it is up to each of us to make the most of the direction.

The third tool is **awareness**. I found the hardest struggle is gaining awareness of how our environment influences us—in particular, the people we surround ourselves with. I do not always pay conscious attention to the fact that the people I spend the most time with are the people that most thoroughly inspire me. Before, I paid attention to how some people were impacting me, but not all. I had allocated too much time to people who were not helping me grow. Making that move forward was difficult. It was extremely hard to extricate myself from some situations, but I found, over time, it has been the best thing for me. Honestly, I think it was the best thing for their growth as well.

About the Author

Gretchen is an intrapreneur turned entrepreneur. After spending the first half of her career in corporate financial services learning how big business is run, she transitioned to the world of startups and has never looked back. As founder of Capital Access for All, Gretchen focuses on helping new startup founders navigate the challenges of building an early-stage business. Whether challenged by raising money, hiring for the team, creating a deliberate culture, or telling their story, Gretchen helps early-stage founders avoid unnecessary mistakes and find the right connections to accelerate their momentum. In addition, Gretchen coaches individuals interested in reinventing themselves to build a new future.

Gretchen co-authored the book *LAUNCH! 11 Key Elements of Wildly Successful Startups*. She is a startup advisor, coach, and angel investor.

You can contact Gretchen through LinkedIn at www.linkedin.com/in/gretchen-wilson-boston/ or find more on her website: www.capitalaccessforall.com.

Conclusion

As you reach the end of this book, our hope as the publishers is that you have been inspired by the incredible people we invited to share insights, stories, tips, and tools for navigating the Clickety-Clack of life and staying peaceful within, even when things around you are seemingly toxic.

You may have noticed we used the word *seemingly* in front of the word *toxic*. This is for a specific purpose. Many of our authors love the world and are able to accept whatever is happening around them, still seeing the world as good. Because they use the tools they shared with you, they are either unphased by outward appearances, or in many cases, the time they stay in the negative passes quickly. Seeing the world as toxic is ultimately a choice. One can look at the same event and see it as toxic, or a challenge, a learning experience, or, as some say, "It is what it is." It's all perspective.

As you read our authors' answers to the three questions, did you feel connected to any of them or their perspectives?

If you connected to any of our contributors in strong and meaningful ways, we suggest you reach out to them. Look up the people, websites, programs, or products they mentioned within their chapter of the book.

Our wish for you—like those we invited to be in this book—is to be a walking, talking demonstration of being able to stay neutral, calm, and peaceful, no matter what is happening in the outside world.

Thank you for reading this book!

Keith Leon S.

Multiple International Award-Winning Author, Speaker, and Publisher

LeonSmithPublishing.com

BeyondBeliefPublishing.com

About the Publisher

In 2004, Babypie Publishing was founded by entrepreneurs Keith and Maura Leon when they decided to self-publish their co-authored book, *The Seven Steps to Successful Relationships*. When Babypie published its second book, Keith Leon's, *Who Do You Think You Are? Discover the Purpose of Your Life*, a few years later—implementing a large marketing campaign that introduced the book to over a million people on the first day it came out—both books became bestsellers overnight.

After the success of their first two titles, Keith and Maura were approached by another author who believed they could take his book to bestseller status as well. They decided to give it a shot, and Warren Henningsen's book, *If I Can You Can: Insights of an Average Man*, became an international bestseller the day it was released.

Before long, Babypie Publishing was receiving manuscript submissions from all over the world and publishing such titles as Ronny K. Prasad's, *Welcome to Your Life;* Melanie Eatherton's, *The 7-Minute Mirror;* and Maribel Jimenez and Keith Leon's,

The Bake Your Book Program: How to Finish Your Book Fast and Serve It Up HOT!

With a vision to make an even greater impact, Babypie Publishing began offering comprehensive writing and publishing programs, as well as a full range of à-la-carte services to support independent authors and innovative professionals in getting their message out in the most powerful and effective manner. In 2015, Keith and Maura developed the YouSpeakIt book program to make it easy, fast, and affordable for busy entrepreneurs and cutting-edge health practitioners to get their mission and message out to the world.

In 2016, Leon Smith Publishing was created as the new home for Babypie, YouSpeakIt, and future projects. In 2018, Beyond Belief Publishing was added as an imprint for spiritual and esoteric titles.

Keith Leon S. has continued to write books, speak, and teach on stages worldwide, and he mentors authors in the easiest, most effective ways to market their mission, message, and books. Keith is a five-time award-winning, seven-time International Bestselling Author who has spoken at events that include Jack Canfield, Bob Proctor, Dr. John Demartini, Neale Donald Walsch, Barbara De Angelis, Dr. John Gray, Dr. Michael Beckwith, Joe Vitale, Marie Diamond, and Marianne Williamson.

Keith has appeared on many popular radio and television broadcasts on ABC, CBS, NBC, and The Jenny McCarthy Show, to name just a few, and his work has been covered by *Inc. Magazine*, *LA Weekly*, *The Huffington Post*, and *Succeed Magazine*.

Whether you're a transformational author looking for writing and publishing services or a visionary leader ready to take your life and work to the next level, we thank you for visiting our website at LeonSmithPublishing.com, and we look forward to serving you.

Made in the USA
Middletown, DE
14 January 2022

58622097R00080